CREATIVE
Cakes for Men

Debbie Brown

MEREHURST

To my father, Ray, for his
generosity of spirit

Reprinted 1999
First published in 1996 by Merehurst Limited
Ferry House, 51-57 Lacy Road, Putney, London SW15 1PR
Text and Cake Designs © Debra Brown 1996
Photographs © Merehurst Limited 1996
ISBN 1 85391 481 9

A catalogue record for this book is available from the British Library.

Edited by Donna Wood
Designed by Maggie Aldred
Photography by Clive Streeter
Illustrations by King & King Design Associates
Typesetting by Peter A. Lovell
Colour separation by Global Colour, Malaysia
Printed in China by Toppan Printing Co., (H.K.) Ltd.

Contents

Basic Recipes

MADEIRA SPONGE CAKE

The secret of a successful novelty cake is to start with a firm yet moist cake which will withstand any cutting and shaping required without crumbling. Because of this, a Madeira recipe is a good choice and it can be flavoured to give variety.

To make a Madeira cake suitable for any of the designs given in this book, first grease and line the bakeware (see chart).

- Sift the flours together.
- Beat the soft margarine and caster (superfine) sugar together until light and fluffy.
- Gradually add the eggs, one at a time, with a spoonful of flour, beating well after each addition.
- Add any flavouring required.
- Fold the remaining flour into the mixture.
- Spoon the mixture into the bakeware. Make a dip in the top with the back of a spoon.
- Bake in the centre of a preheated oven at 160°C (325°F) Gas 3, until a skewer inserted in the centre comes out clean.
- Leave to cool for five minutes, then turn out of bakeware. When cold, store in an airtight container before use.

VARIATIONS

Vanilla Madeira Add 1 tsp of vanilla essence to every 6-egg mixture.

Lemon Madeira Add the grated rind of 1 lemon and/or juice of 1 lemon to every 6-egg mixture.

Chocolate Madeira Mix 2-3 tbsp of unsweetened cocoa powder with 1 tbsp milk to every 6-egg mixture.

Almond Madeira Add 1 tsp of almond esssence to every 6-egg mixture.

BUTTERCREAM

A layer of freshly applied buttercream on the surface of a cake will fill any small gaps and provide a smooth surface on which the sugarpaste can be applied. Buttercream can also be flavoured.

Makes about 500g (1 lb)

125g (4 oz) butter or soft margarine
1 tbsp milk
375g (12 oz) sifted icing (confectioner's) sugar

- Put the butter or soft margarine into a bowl.
- Add the milk and any flavouring.

▲ *The method above yields a sponge cake suitable for carving into any shape – even that of a gorilla!*

▲ *Buttercream is a very versatile filling. It can be coloured and flavoured in a variety of ways.*

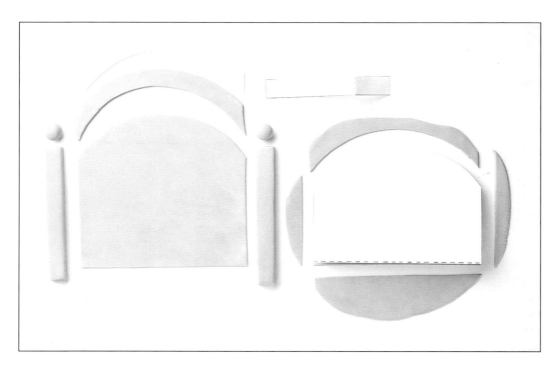

◀ *Pastillage is best for designs where accuracy is important. It will not bend or lose its shape.*

• Sift the icing (confectioner's) sugar into the bowl a little at a time, beating well after each addition, until all the sugar is incorporated and the buttercream has a light, creamy texture.
• Store in an airtight container.

VARIATIONS

Vanilla buttercream Add 1 tsp of vanilla essence.
Lemon buttercream Replace the milk with concentrated lemon juice.
Chocolate buttercream Mix the milk and 2 tbsp of unsweetened cocoa powder to a paste and add to the mixture.
Coffee buttercream Mix the milk and 1 tbsp of coffee to a paste and add to the mixture.

ROYAL ICING

Makes about 280g (9 oz)

1 egg white
250-280g (8-9 oz) sifted icing (confectioner's) sugar

Put the egg white into a bowl. Beat in the sifted icing (confectioner's) sugar, a little at a time, until the icing is firm, glossy and forms peaks when the spoon is pulled out. Cover the bowl with a damp cloth for a few minutes before use.

PASTILLAGE

This paste dries extremely hard, very quickly. It will not bend or lose its shape and is most suitable for precision work.

When using this icing, you do have to work quite quickly as it forms a crust soon after being exposed to the air. Because of this, it is unsuitable for modelling, unless you mix it 50/50 with sugarpaste.

Pastillage can be obtained in high-quality powder form from cake decorating suppliers, but the recipe below is very simple.

Makes about 375g (12 oz)

1 egg white
345g (11 oz) sifted icing (confectioner's) sugar
2 tsp gum tragacanth

• Put the egg white into a bowl and add 280g (9 oz) of the sifted icing (confectioner's) sugar a little at a time, mixing well after each addition.
• Sprinkle the gum tragacanth over the top and put aside for 10 minutes.
• Turn out onto a surface and knead in the remaining icing (confectioner's) sugar.
• Double wrap in polythene or clingfilm (plastic wrap) and store in an airtight container until required.

QUANTITIES CHART

Cake Designs	American Football (page 24)	Decorating Time (page 46)	Bathing Beauties (page 10)	Breakfast Tray (page 39)	Attic Railway (page 21) Massage Parlour (page 36) Artist's Palette (page 17)
Bakeware	Split mix between 18cm (7 in) round tin & 2 ltr (4 pint) ovenproof bowl	25cm (10 in) square tin	25 x 36cm (10 x 14 in) oblong tin	30 x 20cm (12 x 8 in) oblong tin	20cm (8 in) square tin
Self-raising flour	440g (14 oz)	440g (14 oz)	560g (1 lb 2 oz)	375g (12 oz)	250g (8 oz)
Plain flour	220g (7 oz)	220g (7 oz)	280g (9 oz)	185g (6 oz)	125g (4 oz)
Soft margarine	440g (14 oz)	440g (14 oz)	560g (1 lb 2 oz)	375g (12 oz)	250g (8 oz)
Caster (superfine) sugar	440g (14 oz)	440g (14 oz)	560g (1 lb 2 oz)	375g (12 oz)	250g (8 oz)
Eggs, size 2	7	7	9	6	4
Cooking time	1-1¼ hours	1-1¼ hours	1-1¼ hours	1 hour	50 minutes

SUGAR GLUE

All the cake designs in this book depend on sugar glue to stick the components together. An edible glue can be made in a variety of ways, depending on what ingredients are to hand.

Cooled boiled water will stick sugar together, but is not strong enough for modelled pieces that defy gravity! Egg white is a good edible glue, as is royal icing, or a mixture of any paste diluted with a few drops of water. To make an extra-strong glue, mix pastillage or modelling paste, which both have a gum additive, with egg white.

To stick sugar items together, you need only slightly dampen the paste surface with sugar glue. If you apply too much, your modelled piece may slide out of place. Gently press in position, holding for a few moments. Always have some small pieces of foam sponge to hand when creating a novelty cake, as these can be used to support glued modelled pieces whilst drying if necessary.

MODELLING PASTE

Modelling paste is sugarpaste with a gum additive. When the gum is incorporated, it makes the paste

Early Morning Call (page 55) Chaos in the Kitchen (page 73)	Rugby Tackle (page 49) Squash Court Star (page 52) Vintage Car (page 26) Bathroom Sink (page 67) All Too Much (page 60) Couch Potato (page 32)	Plane Favourite (page 30)	We are the Champions! (page 43) Ketchup Lips (page 14)	All Jogged Out (page 64)	Monkey Business (page 70)
20cm (8 in) square tin	25cm (10 in) square tin	2 x 1 ltr (2 pint) ovenproof bowls	20cm (8 in) round tin	25cm (10 in) round tin	Split mix between 2 x 150ml (¼ pint), ¾ ltr (1¼ pint) and 2 ltr (4 pint) ovenproof bowls
315g (10 oz)	375g (12 oz)	375g (12 oz)	375g (12 oz)	440g (14 oz)	440g (14 oz)
155g (5 oz)	185g (6 oz)	185g (6 oz)	185g (6 oz)	220g (7 oz)	220g (7 oz)
315g (10 oz)	375g (12 oz)	375g (12 oz)	375g (12 oz)	440g (14 oz)	440g (14 oz)
315g (10 oz)	375g (12 oz)	375g (12 oz)	375g (12 oz)	440g (14 oz)	440g (14 oz)
5	6	6	6	7	7
1 hour	1 hour	1¼-1½ hours	1¼ hours	1¼ hours	35 minutes (150ml) 1 hour (¾ ltr) 1½ hours (2 ltr)

firm but pliable so it is easier to work with. The modelled items will dry harder and also keep their shape.

There is a natural gum called gum tragacanth which is widely used in the food industry and a new man-made alternative called carboxy methyl cellulose (CMC) which is cheaper than gum tragacanth and also goes further.

However, if you do not want to make your own modelling paste before embarking on the projects in this book, there are some ready made modelling pastes available that give good results. Even more

useful, they can also be obtained pre-coloured.

All items are available from cake decorating suppliers.

Makes about 500g (1 lb)

2 tsp gum tragacanth
500g (1 lb) sugarpaste

Put the gum tragacanth onto a work surface and knead into the sugarpaste. Double wrap the resulting modelling paste in polythene or clingfilm (plastic wrap) and store in an airtight container for a few hours before use.

Modelling Techniques

SIMPLE FACES

Below and right are ten different faces created from the same modelling technique. On some, modelling paste has been used for hair as well as royal icing, to show that different mediums can be used successfully.

These modelled faces are extremely easy to make. Any one you model will look different from the last, even if you choose the same expressions. Just by minutely moving a feature, or slightly altering the face shape, you can make your model unique.

Eyebrows are important for expression. The higher you draw them the more innocent and open the faces look. Just moving the eyebrows to a slant without changing anything else, gives a completely different facial expression (see above).

If you want to make a duplicate of someone you know, start by copying their hair colour and style. Then, note anything obvious like facial hair, glasses, and so on. Because the remaining features are so simply done, a combination of the more obvious will ensure the recipient will know who's who!

HINTS AND TIPS

• If your cake has to be cut into shapes, store it in an airtight container for at least six hours before use to allow the texture to settle.

• A sharp serrated knife is best for cake cutting and trimming, but a sharp plain-edged knife is best for cutting paste. To avoid paste 'pulling' when cut, do not draw the knife through the paste, but cut cleanly downwards.

• After the buttercream is spread on the surface of the cake, it may begin to set before you apply the sugarpaste. Simply rework the buttercream with a knife or apply a little more.

• Wear plastic gloves when kneading the colours into paste as the food colouring may stain your hands.

- To avoid undue mess and to regulate amounts, apply food colourings to all icing using cocktail sticks (toothpicks).
- Knead the paste until warm and pliable before use.
- Use icing (confectioner's) sugar when rolling out paste and keep moving the paste around to prevent sticking.
- Roll the sugarpaste to a thickness of 3-4mm (⅛ in) unless otherwise stated.
- When a large piece of sugarpaste is rolled out, lift by folding over the rolling pin. This will make it easier to position.
- To obtain a smooth surface on sugarpaste, rub gently with a cake smoother.
- You may wish to remove the piece of sugarpaste from the cakeboard on which the cake will sit. Because the cake is moist, the sugarpaste underneath has a tendency to become slightly sticky.
- When the sugarpaste is dry, polish the surface with your hands to remove excess icing (confectioner's) sugar and to give a sheen.
- Keep coloured icings separate as colours may bleed into others when stored.
- Sugarpaste-covered cakeboards are best left to dry for 12 hours before use. If the cakeboard is needed before, add ½ tsp of gum tragacanth or similar additive to the sugarpaste so the board will dry harder much quicker.
- Always store paste icing in an airtight container and/or polythene bags.
- Thoroughly remove excess icing (confectioner's) sugar from the surface of dried paste before attempting any painting or drawing, as the colours may spread.
- Food colourings can be diluted with either clear alcohol (gin or vodka) or water for painting. Use clear alcohol in preference as this evaporates more quickly.
- When choosing ribbon for the cakeboard banding, remember you need a slightly thicker width if you sugarpaste the cakeboard.
- Store the finished cake in a cardboard box in a warm dry room. NEVER store in the refrigerator, the atmosphere is damp and the cake will spoil.
- If you hate waste, mix leftover cake crumbs and buttercream together to make a truffle paste. You can colour this to match the cake.

Bathing Beauties

This cheeky cake will remind your man that you both need a holiday in the sun!

CAKE AND DECORATION
25 x 36cm (10 x 14 in) oblong cake (page 6)
625g (1¼ lb) buttercream (page 4) · 1.125kg (2¼ lb) sugarpaste · egg yellow, pink, black, blue, flesh and brown food colouring pastes · sugar glue (page 6) · 90g (3 oz) pastillage (page 5)
250g (8 oz) modelling paste (page 6) · 45g (1½ oz) royal icing (page 5) · black and blue food colouring pens · 315g (10 oz) piping gel

EQUIPMENT
25 x 36cm (10 x 14 in) oblong cakeboard · sheet of card · cocktail sticks (toothpicks) · 2.5cm (1 in) square cutter · fine paintbrush · lined rolling pin pieces of foam sponge · no. 2 and no. 4 piping tubes (tips) · waxed paper · 3cm (1½ in) circle cutter

1 Cut the top from the cake where it has risen and trim off the crust. Cut a layer in the cake and sandwich back together using 375g (12 oz) buttercream. Position the cake on the cakeboard.

2 Using the sheet of card, make the pool template (see page 78). Position the template on top of the cake. Cut around the outside, removing the top layer only. Using the remaining

▲ *Leave a space for the steps when you apply the strip to the pool side.*

buttercream, spread a layer over the surface of the cake.

3 Roll out 200g (6½ oz) white sugarpaste. Cut out the pool shape using the template, then position on the cake. To cover the pool sides, roll out 125g (4 oz) and cut a strip the depth of the pool and position around the inside edge. Smooth the join closed.

4 Colour 500g (1 lb) sugarpaste cream using a little egg yellow. Using 345g (11 oz), roll out and cut strips to cover the four sides of the cake, keeping the sharp corners.

5 Split 280g (9 oz) sugarpaste into quarters. Colour one piece pink, another pale pink, the third piece beige using a touch each of egg yellow and black, and the last piece grey. Using a 2.5cm (1 in) square cutter, roll out each colour and cut the tiles for the top of the cake. Roll out 90g (3 oz) cream sugarpaste and cut more tiles. Position all the tiles on the cake, trimming around the pool edge.

6 Using the remaining cream sugarpaste, roll out and cut the strip for the pool edge, leaving space for the

pool steps. Stick in place using a little sugar glue.

7 Using pastillage, make two sets of steps, four step rails, the diving board and the newspaper with a spy hole. When the icing has formed a crust, stick the steps, rails and base of the diving board in place. Set the diving board and newspaper aside to dry.

8 Colour 45g (1½ oz) modelling paste blue. Make two towels, one using the lined rolling pin and the other by marking a line at either end using a knife. Place the lined towel on the cake and roll up the other for the pillow, sticking in place with a little sugar glue. Reserve the trimmings. Make another rolled towel using grey paste trimmings.

9 Colour 22g (¾ oz) modelling paste lilac using a little blue and pink food colouring pastes, and make a third towel. Reserve the trimmings. Colour another 22g (¾ oz) pale blue and make the last towel.

10 Colour 100g (3½ oz) modelling paste flesh colour. Split into four equal-sized pieces and model the figures using the photograph on page 13 as a guide. Make the man's shorts from the lilac trimmings.

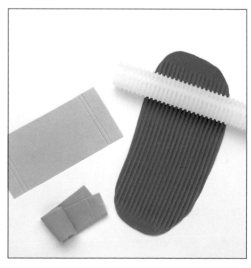

▲ *The man's towel is textured with the pin; the others simply marked at each end.*

◀ *Each figure is made from a sausage shape, cut and moulded as shown. The floating girl's hair is piped onto waxed paper.*

Stick each figure in their pose using a little sugar glue. If necessary, use pieces of foam for support. Mark their smiles with the tip of a no. 4 piping tube.

11 Colour 30g (1 oz) royal icing cream. Pipe the blonde hair on the paddling girl using a no. 4 piping tube. Put a piece of waxed paper under the floating girl's head. Pipe the hair cascading outwards using a no. 2 piping tube and leave to dry. Colour the remaining royal icing brown and pipe the hair on the third girl using a no. 4 piping tube.

12 Using 30g (1 oz) white modelling paste, cut out the four lifebelts using a 3cm (1½ in) circle cutter, then remove the centre of each using the end of a piping tube. With blue modelling paste trimmings, cut two small triangles for each lifebelt and stick in place. Stick the lifebelts onto the sides of the cake.

13 Using the remaining modelling paste, make the kerchief for the man's head and two sets of tiny eyes for the girls. Colour some trimmings pale lilac, pink and black. Model the swimsuits and sunglasses. Stick every-

thing in place, including the diving board, and leave the cake to dry.

14 Using the black food colouring pen, draw the newspaper print, sticking in place with a little sugar glue. Draw the eyes using the pens.

15 Colour the piping gel pale blue. Spoon into the pool and swirl around the girls' legs. Rest the floating girl on the gel and press down gently. Wipe a little gel around the pool edge.

▼ *Colour the piping gel pale blue and spoon it into the pool to represent water on the day of the presentation.*

Ketchup Lips

The way to a man's heart is through his stomach, so give him this luscious-lipped burger.

CAKE AND DECORATION
20cm (8 in) round cake (page 7) · 1.065kg
(2 lb 2 oz) sugarpaste · bright blue, brown, egg
yellow, green, dark green, red and black food
colouring pastes · 440g (14 oz) buttercream (page
4) · clear alcohol (gin or vodka) · 282g (9¼ oz)
modelling paste (page 6) · sugar glue (page 6)
100g (3½ oz) soft royal icing (page 5)
confectioner's glaze

EQUIPMENT
36cm (14 in) oval cakeboard · ruler · fine
and medium paintbrushes · cocktail sticks
(toothpicks) · no. 2 plain piping tube (tip)
greaseproof paper piping bag

TIP
*Confectioner's
glaze is useful for
giving food items
a greasy look.*

1 Colour 440g (14 oz) sugarpaste
bright blue. Roll out and cover the
cakeboard. Reserve the trimmings. Trim
the crust from the cake, keeping the top
rounded.

2 For the burger, cut two layers in
the centre of the cake, 1cm (½ in)
apart. Using three-quarters of the
buttercream, spread a layer over the
top of the burger and on the top of the
bun base. Spread the remainder thinly
over the surface of the cake.

3 Colour 125g (4 oz) sugarpaste
brown. Roll out and cut a long
strip measuring at least 60cm (24 in) in
length, and place around the edge of the
burger, smoothing at the top and
bottom in line with the surface of the
cake. Using a knife, indent all the
uneven lines and marks. Water down a
little brown food colouring with 1 tsp
clear alcohol. Using a medium
paintbrush, paint over the surface of
the burger, then set aside to dry.

▲ *Mark the burger with a knife, then
paint with diluted brown food colouring.*

4 Colour 500g (1 lb) sugarpaste
golden brown using egg yellow
with a touch of brown. Roll out 375g
(12 oz) and cover the top of the bun
completely, smoothing the sugarpaste
underneath to round off the edge. Place
the bap base onto the centre of the
cakeboard. With the remaining golden
brown paste, roll out and cut a strip
60cm (24 in) in length and cover the
outer edge of the bun base.

5 To make the lettuce, colour 45g
(1½ oz) modelling paste pale green.
Thinly roll out and cut into strips. Roll
the rolling pin over one edge to thin
and frill, gather up and stick in position
around the top edge of the bun base.

6 Colour 30g (1 oz) modelling paste
dark green and model three rough
circles for the gherkin slices. Mark the
outer edge of each with a knife, then

stick in position evenly spaced around the top edge of the bun base. Carefully lift the burger and position on the bun base.

7 To make the mayonnaise, colour royal icing cream using a touch of egg yellow. Reserve 30g (1 oz) for later. Carefully spoon the remainder over the edge of the burger letting it drip down the sides. Put the top of the bap in place before it has time to set.

8 Colour 170g (5½ oz) modelling paste cream using a touch of egg yellow. Split in half. Thickly roll out

▶ *Once the bun base and top are covered, make lettuce by frilling green sugarpaste strips.*

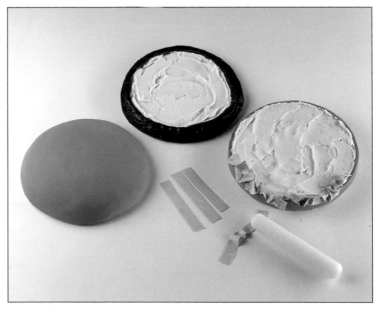

one piece and cut nine chips. Stick two chips in position for the legs and pinch the ends to make the feet. With the remaining half, model the two arms and stick in position.

9 Make the lips using 22g (¾ oz) modelling paste coloured bright red. Mark the creases with a cocktail stick and stick in place on the front of the burger.

10 Dilute a little green food colouring paste with a few drops of clear alcohol. Using a fine paintbrush, paint a thin coat over the lettuce and gherkin slices. In separate bowls, dilute a little egg yellow and brown food colouring paste with a few drops of clear alcohol. Using a fine paintbrush, paint a little of each colour over the chips.

11 Take 15g (½ oz) white modelling paste and halve it. Model the two eyes with the first piece, then colour the remaining piece black and make the pupils and eyelashes. Make the iris with some of the bright blue sugarpaste trimmings and stick in place.

12 Using the no. 2 piping tube and the remaining cream royal icing, pipe the sesame seeds over the top of the bap. Pipe two minute marks on each eye to give them a sparkle.

13 Using a medium paintbrush and a little confectioner's glaze, paint a thin coat over the mayonnaise drips, burger, ketchup lips, lettuce, gherkin slices and the chips to give them a greasy look. When everything is dry, position the chips in the burger's hand and on the cakeboard.

▶ *Make the chips and the burger's arms from the same piece of modelling paste. Mark creases on the lips with a cocktail stick.*

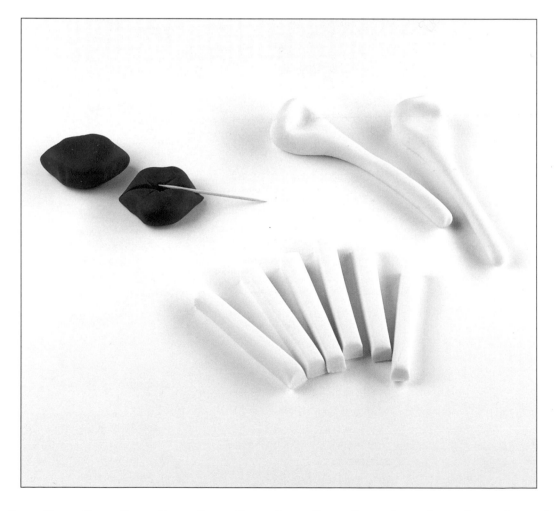

Artist's Palette

Inspire your old master by presenting him with this priceless work of art.

CAKE AND DECORATION

20cm (8 in) square cake (page 6) · 775g (1 lb 9 oz) modelling paste (page 6) · 1.125kg (2 lb 4 oz) sugarpaste · 375g (12 oz) pastillage (page 5) 375g (12 oz) buttercream (page 4) · brown, egg yellow, chestnut, black, red, orange, peach, yellow, green, jade green, dark green and navy food colouring pastes · clear alcohol (gin or vodka) · icing (confectioner's) sugar · brilliant silver lustre powder · sugar glue (page 6) · 100g (3½ oz) royal icing (page 5) · 1 tbsp piping gel

EQUIPMENT

40 x 30cm (16 x 12 in) oblong cakeboard · cake smoother · piece of voile or netting · large sheet of card · 2.5cm (1 in) circle cutter · cocktail sticks (toothpicks) · ruler · fine and medium paintbrushes · tall and medium glasses or pots miniature circle cutters · 3 greaseproof paper piping bags

1 As the sides of the cakeboard are covered to make the canvas, knead 375g (12 oz) each of modelling paste and sugarpaste together to make a slightly stronger paste. Roll out and cover the cakeboard completely, trimming around the base. Using the cake smoother, press a piece of voile or netting over the surface to resemble the texture of canvas, then set aside to dry.

2 Make the template for the palette using the sheet of card (see page 78). Colour the pastillage pale brown. Using the template as a guide, thinly roll out and cut the palette shape. Work as quickly as you can as this icing dries fast. Cut the circle from the palette using the 2.5cm (1 in) circle cutter. Reserve the pastillage trimmings.

3 Dilute a little brown and egg yellow food colouring pastes with 1 tbsp clear alcohol. To get the wood effect, paint on a thin coat of colour using the medium paintbrush. Keep the brush quite dry to encourage the streaks. Leave the palette to dry on a completely flat surface.

▲ *The pastillage palette is painted with a thin coat of colour to resemble woodgrain.*

4 Slice the top off the cake where it has risen and trim off the crust. Cut the cake exactly in half and sandwich one on top of the other using half the buttercream. Spread the remainder over the surface of the cake.

5 Colour 750g (1½ lb) sugarpaste brown and roll out. Place the end of the cake down onto it and cut around. Cover the opposite end in the

▲ Cover the cake with buttercream then apply brown sugarpaste in neat sections. Scratch on wavy lines using a cocktail stick.

same way, then the back and front, and finally the top. Using a ruler or similar straight edge, indent a deep line around the box for the lid. Scratch wavy lines onto the surface for the woodgrain using a cocktail stick.

6 Dilute a little brown food colouring paste with 1 tbsp clear alcohol. Using the medium paintbrush, paint over the box to highlight the woodgrain. Set aside to dry.

7 Colour 125g (4 oz) modelling paste chestnut. Dust the inside of a tall glass or pot with icing sugar. Push the chestnut modelling paste into the glass and work the paste around the inside, moving constantly to stop the paste sticking. Trim the top, remove from the glass and set aside to dry. Reserve the trimmings. Colour 75g (2½ oz) modelling paste cream using a little egg yellow and make another pot as before, using the smaller container.

8 To make the paintbrushes, colour the brown pastillage trimmings and make two black, one red, one orange and four brown. Roll long thin sausage shapes tapering at one end and cut the tops straight. Indent the lines around each brush using a knife. Make the eight brush heads with pastillage trimmings coloured brown. Set everything aside to dry.

▲ *The paint pots are modelled from drinking tumblers; the paintbrushes from long sausages of pastillage.*

9 Split 185g (6 oz) modelling paste into five equal pieces and make the paint tubes. Roll one end of each to form the top and flatten the bottom, cut straight and mark small lines for the seal using a cocktail stick. With the trimmings, model the five lids. Indent the centre of each lid using the miniature circle cutters, marking the lines around the edge with a cocktail stick. Colour a little of the remaining modelling paste dark orange, orange,

peach, yellow and light brown and cut the colour strips for each tube.

10 Mix a little brilliant silver lustre powder with a few drops of clear alcohol. Using a fine paintbrush, paint a thin coat over the tops of the paintbrushes and paint tubes. Leave to dry, then repeat.

11 Position the cake on the cakeboard with the palette in front. Stick pots, paint tubes and the two paintbrushes in place.

12 Colour small amounts of the royal icing using a mixture of food colouring pastes. Put the yellow, peach and dark orange royal icing into separate piping bags, cut a hole in the tip of each and pipe the 'paint' on the tubes and the palette. Keeping similar colours grouped together, spread the remaining coloured royal icing onto the palette with a knife.

13 When the cake is ready for presentation, spoon the piping gel into the small pot for the water and arrange the paintbrushes in the larger pot.

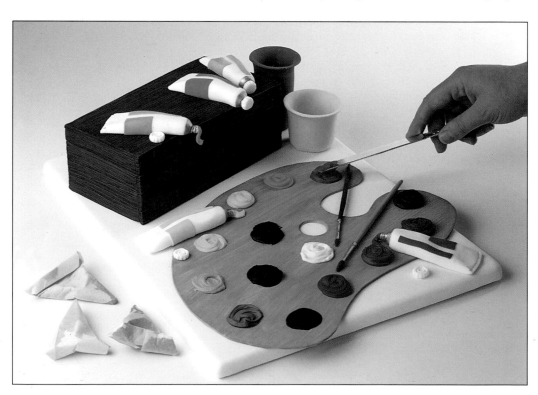

▶ *Spread the remaining 'paint' swirls onto the palette using a knife.*

Attic Railway

Like father, like son – if the male members of your family are train set mad you will recognize this scene. Poor teddy is now redundant!

CAKE AND DECORATION
20cm (8 in) square cake (page 6) · 1.125kg
(2 lb 4 oz) sugarpaste · brown, sage green, black,
blue, flesh, bright green, egg yellow, orange and
red food colouring pastes · clear alcohol (gin or
vodka) · 250g (8 oz) buttercream (page 4) · 45g
(1½ oz) royal icing (page 5) · 500g (1 lb)
modelling paste (page 6) · sugar glue (page 6)
black and blue food colouring pens

EQUIPMENT
30cm (12 in) hexagonal cakeboard · cocktail sticks
(toothpicks) · ruler · no. 2, 3 and 4 piping tubes
(tips) · fine and medium paintbrushes
sheet of greaseproof paper · shell piping
tube (tip)

1 Colour 375g (12 oz) sugarpaste dark brown. Roll out and cover the cakeboard. Indent the lines for the floorboards with a ruler and mark the end of each plank with a knife and the nails with the tip of a no. 3 piping tube. Mark the woodgrain pattern with a cocktail stick. Dilute a little brown food colouring paste with 1 tbsp clear alcohol. Using the medium paintbrush, paint a colour wash over the floorboards to highlight the woodgrain and put aside to dry.

2 Cut the top from the cake where it has risen and trim off the crust. Cut the cake exactly in half and sandwich one on top of the other using half the buttercream. Using the remaining buttercream, spread a layer over the surface of the cake. Position the cake on the cakeboard.

3 Colour the remaining sugarpaste sage green. Roll out and cut an oblong measuring 36 x 25cm (14 x 10 in) for the tablecloth. Trim each corner to round off, lift and place over the cake, encouraging pleats.

4 Trace the railway track outline onto the sheet of greaseproof paper (see page 78). Scribe the outline on the top of the cake using a cocktail stick. Indent the sleepers for under the rail using a knife. Colour half the royal icing black. To make the rails, pipe over the scribed track outline with a no. 2 piping tube.

5 Colour 22g (¾ oz) modelling paste black. Using half, model two pairs of shoes, one pair slightly larger for Dad. Colour 75g (2½ oz) modelling paste blue. Use 30g (1 oz) for Dad's trousers and 15g (½ oz) for the boy's trousers. Using 7g (¼ oz), model the four train carriages. With the remainder make the train engine, wheels, carriage roofs, tunnel and teddy's tiny nose. Put the nose aside, then stick everything in place using a little sugar glue.

6 Using the photograph as a guide, make the two tops for father and son, again one slightly larger than the other, with half the white modelling paste. Colour 75g (2½ oz) modelling paste flesh. Using a 15g (¼ oz) piece, make two heads, two tiny noses and four hands. Indent the smiles with the tip of a no. 4 piping tube. Model a box with the remaining piece, marking the

▲ *The two figures are made from the same components but one is much larger than the other.*

▶ *The detail is drawn on the books and boxes with a food colouring pen.*

streaky and roll the ball. Stick everything in place.

8 Colour 22g (¾ oz) modelling paste grey using a touch of the black food colouring paste. Make the station, two houses, two huts and the platform. Model three little chimneys. Cover the tunnel with tiny pieces to look like stones and make extra to scatter around the tunnel. Put the chimneys aside, then stick everything in place using a little sugar glue.

9 Split 60g (2 oz) modelling paste and colour different shades of green. Cover two more books, then model the bushes and trees using a little sugar glue to stick in position. Repeatedly press the tip of a shell piping tube into the bushes, to give texture.

10 Colour 125g (4 oz) modelling paste beige using a touch each of egg yellow and brown. Make the three cardboard boxes, marking the closed lids with a knife, one skittle and two book covers. Stick in place using a little sugar glue.

11 Colour 22g (¾ oz) modelling paste rust, using a touch each of the orange and brown. Make all the

lid with a knife, and stick everything in place.

7 Using the remaining white modelling paste, make the eyes and the pages for seven books. With the remaining blue modelling paste, make a skittle and the covers of two books. Knead a little each of the white and blue modelling paste together until

roofs, sticking the chimneys on top. Make the teddy, sticking the black nose in place, and model the ball. Colour the remaining modelling paste red to make the remaining skittle and cover the last book pages. Stick in place.

12 Colour the remaining royal icing brown with a touch of orange. Pipe the hair with the no. 4 piping tube. Leave the cake to dry thoroughly.

13 Using the black and blue food colouring pens, draw the eyes and eyebrows. Add the lettering, cobweb, teddy's eyes and all the windows and doors using the black food colouring pen.

◀ *The figures can be personalized to suit the cake recipient, if wished.*

23

American Football

American football fans will love this reminder of their favourite Stars and Stripes game.

CAKE AND DECORATION

18cm (7 in) round cake and 2ltr (4 pint) bowl-shaped cake (page 6) · 1.42kg (2 lb 14 oz) sugarpaste · blue and black food colouring pastes 500g (1 lb) buttercream (page 4) · sugar glue (page 6) · 100g (3½ oz) pastillage (page 5) brilliant silver lustre powder · clear alcohol (gin or vodka)

EQUIPMENT

30cm (12 in) round cakeboard · cocktail sticks (toothpicks) · medium and large star cutters 5cm (2 in) circle cutter · piping tube (tip) fine and medium paintbrushes

1 Colour 1.1kg (2 lb 3½ oz) sugarpaste blue/grey using a touch of blue and black. Roll out 375g (12 oz) and cover the cakeboard. Cut out stars with the medium cutter.

2 Cut the tops from each cake where they have risen and trim off the crust. Put the bowl cake on top of the round cake. Cut out the opening at the front 13cm (5 in) wide and 8cm (3½ in) high, to a depth of 1cm (½ in). Trim the base at an inward angle and trim each side of the helmet to flatten slightly.

3 Spread half the buttercream in the layer, then spread the remainder in a thin layer over the surface of the cake.

4 Colour 140g (4½ oz) sugarpaste black. Roll out half and cover the recess on the front of the helmet. With the remainder cut a 30cm (12 in) strip and wrap around the base of the helmet at the back. Cut two circles with the cutter and position either side of the helmet. Place the cake on the board.

5 Using 45g (1½ oz) blue/grey sugarpaste, pad the top of the helmet to make it more rounded. Roll out the remaining blue/grey paste and cover the helmet, stretching and smoothing down to remove the pleats. Cut around the recess and the curve at the back, and trim at the base. Using the end of a piping tube, cut out two

▲ *Stick the two cakes together with butter-cream and trim to the shape of the helmet.*

▲ *Cover the front recess with black sugarpaste. Add a base strip and two side circles.*

circles either side of the helmet to expose the black paste underneath. Model four small flattened ball shapes and stick two each side.

6 Cut a white sugarpaste strip and stick around the edge of the recess. Cut two squares, the first measuring 5cm (2 in), the second slightly smaller, and stick on the front of the helmet, the smaller on top of the larger underneath. Thinly roll and cut a strip for the top measuring 2.5cm x 32cm (1 x 12½ in). Reserve the trimmings.

7 Colour 100g (3½ oz) sugarpaste dusky blue, using the blue with a touch of black. Cut out the stars for the cakeboard using a medium cutter and two stars for either side of the helmet using a large star cutter. Cut two long strips for the top of the helmet.

8 To make the helmet frame, roll a pastillage sausage and stick in place resting on the board, curving up to the top of the recess. Hold in position until the pastillage sets. Roll another sausage for the top piece and stick in position. Roll out the centre piece and lay over the bottom piece curving up and joining at the top. Make two small sausages and stick in place supporting the centre piece. With the white trimmings, cut two strips and stick over the top piece. Make the two screws and stick in position, marking with a cocktail stick.

9 When dry, mix brilliant silver lustre powder and 2 tsp clear alcohol to a paste. Paint a thin edge of silver around each star and a thin coat over the helmet frame and two screws.

TIP

Use the fine paintbrush to paint the silver edges around the stars and the medium paintbrush to paint the helmet frame and screws. Leave to dry for 10 minutes before applying another coat.

Vintage Car

This tasty classic will be the most coveted of his collection.

CAKE AND DECORATION

25cm (10 in) square cake (page 7) · 1.125kg (2 lb 4 oz) sugarpaste · 625g (1¼ lb) buttercream (page 4) · black food colouring paste · 595g (1 lb 3 oz) modelling paste (page 6) · clear alcohol (gin or vodka) · brilliant silver lustre powder sugar glue (page 6) · 15g (½ oz) royal icing (page 5) · black food colouring pen confectioner's glaze

EQUIPMENT

36 x 25cm (14 x 10 in) oblong cakeboard cocktail sticks (toothpicks) · ruler · fine and medium paintbrushes · 3.5cm (1¼ in), 3.2cm (1⅛ in) and miniature circle cutters · pieces of foam sponge · no. 2 piping tube (tip)

1 Roll out 410g (13 oz) sugarpaste and cover the cakeboard. Set aside to dry. Cut the top from the cake where it has risen and trim off the crust. Cut a 5cm (2 in) strip from one side of the cake, then cut this strip exactly in half. Cut the remaining cake in half and sandwich one on top of the other using one third of the buttercream. Sandwich the two small cakes side-by-side onto the top of the large cake.

2 Trim the top of the cab to slope downwards from the back and trim off the edge at the back to round off. Trim the front of the car on either side

▲ *Cut and assemble the cake pieces into a basic car shape, trimming the cab to slope downwards.*

▼ *The back view of the car. Number-plates could be personalized.*

to narrow and round off the grille, sloping the bonnet slightly downwards from the windscreen. To lengthen the cab, thickly roll out 45g (1½ oz) sugarpaste and cut a piece to fit the front windscreen, sticking in place with a little buttercream. Position the cake on the cakeboard. Using the remaining buttercream, spread a layer over the surface of the cake.

3 Colour 375g (12 oz) sugarpaste black. Roll out 125g (4 oz) and cut a strip to fit around the base of the car, 2.5cm (1 in) in width. Roll the strip up, position one end on the base of the car, then unroll the strip around the cake, rubbing the join closed.

4 To cover the top of the cab, roll out 100g (3½ oz) black sugarpaste and cut a piece to fit. To cover the front, back and sides of the cab, thinly roll out the remaining black sugarpaste and cut pieces to fit, 5cm (2 in) in depth. Cut the front piece with a curve to follow the line of the bonnet.

5 To cover the sides and back of the car, roll out the remaining white sugarpaste and cut out a 56cm (22 in) long strip. Measure the uncovered cake from the cab to the black strip around the base of the car and cut the width required. Wrap round the back of the car, covering the sides, leaving the front uncovered. Roll out and cut a piece for the top to make the bonnet. Indent the lines with a knife.

6 To make the grille, cover the front of the car with 30g (1 oz) modelling paste. Mark the criss-cross lines with a knife. Mix 1 tsp clear alcohol with a little brilliant silver lustre powder. Using the medium paintbrush, stipple a thin coat over the sides of the cab.

7 Colour 410g (13 oz) modelling paste black. Split a 140g (4½ oz) piece into six and model the tyres, marking a criss-cross pattern for the tread using a knife. With 60g (2 oz) white modelling paste, make the wheel spokes and rim using circle cutters and the photograph as a guide. Assemble together, then stick the four main wheels in position on the cake.

8 Using 125g (4 oz) black modelling paste, make the four wheel guards, two with running boards,

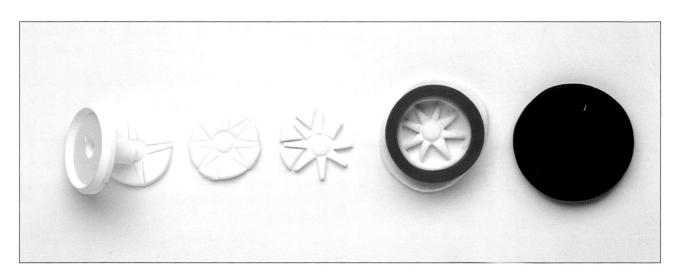

and stick in place. Support with pieces of foam whilst drying. Stick the two spare wheels in position using a little sugar glue. To support the front bumper, cut a thick oblong to fit between the two front wheels using 22g (3/4 oz) black paste. With the trimmings, roll out and cut a circle using the 3.5cm (1 1/4 in) cutter. Cut this circle into quarters, then stick two of the pieces against the grille. To support the back bumper, cut another thick oblong the width of the car back, using a further 22g (3/4 oz) paste and stick in place.

9 Using the remaining black paste, cut out the window frames for the two sides, the back and the windscreen. Stick in place, then indent the lines around each window with a knife.

10 With the remaining white modelling paste, make the two licence plates, the front and back bumpers, the headlights, six side lights (four on the front), the brake lights for the back, the emblem for the grille, the cab roof trims, and the six hubs for each wheel, indenting the centres of each with the miniature circle cutter and the tip of the no. 2 piping tube. Roll out and cut strips for the two running boards, indenting the lines with a knife.

11 With royal icing and a no. 2 piping tube, pipe the windscreen wipers, the door handles and hinges, and the coach line on the edge of each wheel guard.

12 Mix 2 tsp clear alcohol with brilliant silver lustre powder to make a paste. Paint a thin coat over all the car details, leave to dry, then add a further thin coat. When completely dry, draw the line detail on the car and the edge of the cakeboard using the black food colouring pen.

13 To give the car its shine, paint a thin coat of confectioner's glaze over the cab, windows and wheel guards using the medium paintbrush. Leave to dry, then paint another thin coat over the cab frame only.

▲ *The wheel spokes and rim are made with the cutters. Mark the black paste tyres with a knife to resemble tread.*

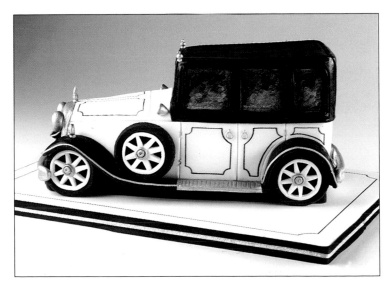

Plane Favourite

The party is sure to take off when this supersonic cake lands on the table!

CAKE AND DECORATION
2 x 1ltr (2 pint) bowl cakes (page 7) · 1.85kg (3¾ lb) sugarpaste · blue and pink food colouring paste · clear alcohol (gin or vodka) · 345g (11 oz) pastillage (page 5) · 345g (11 oz) buttercream (page 4) · black, red and blue food colouring pens · 45g (1½ oz) royal icing (page 5)

EQUIPMENT
40cm (16 in) round cakeboard · cocktail sticks (toothpicks) · medium paintbrush · sheet of card no. 3 plain piping tube (tip) · greaseproof paper piping bag · pieces of foam sponge

---

1 Cover the cakeboard using 625g (1¼ lb) white sugarpaste. Dilute a little blue food colouring paste with clear alcohol. Using the paintbrush, paint the sky effect on one side of the cakeboard, fading out to the centre. Add a tiny amount of the pink food colouring to achieve a different hue. Leave to dry.

2 Make the templates for the wings and fin using the sheet of card (see page 79). Only one wing template is required as the reverse is used to make the second wing.

3 To make the plane's fuselage, knead 200g (6½ oz) pastillage until warm and pliable and roll a thick sausage 38cm (15 in) in length, tapering at either end for the nose and tail. Using the remaining pastillage and the card templates, make the two wings and the fin. Make one piece at a time, marking the detail on each wing with a knife. Leave the pastillage pieces to dry for at least 24 hours.

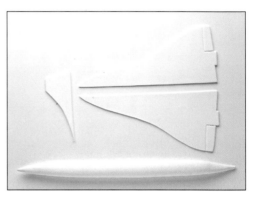

▲ *The wings, fin, nose and tail are made from pastillage and left to dry overnight.*

4 Cut the cake into pieces and group close together on the unpainted side of the cakeboard. Spread buttercream over the surface of the cake.

5 To make the cloud, thickly roll out the remaining sugarpaste and cover the cake, smoothing some over the side of the cakeboard.

6 When the pastillage pieces for the plane are completely dry, draw the cockpit windows, small dots for the windows and the engine rear on each wing using the black food colouring pen. With the red and blue food colouring pens, draw the logo.

7 Using the royal icing and the piping tube, assemble the plane in position using the foam pieces for support whilst drying. Finally, draw the birds on the cakeboard using the black food colouring pen.

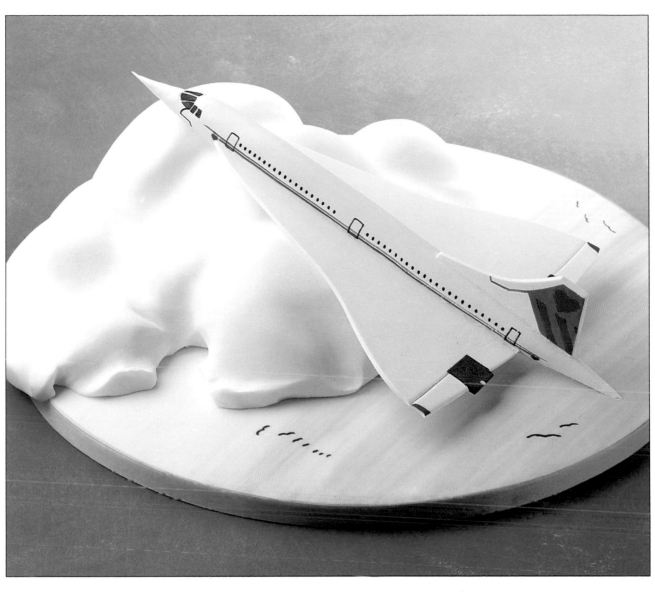

▶ Group the cake pieces on the unpainted side of the cakeboard to make the clouds.

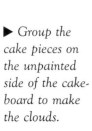

TIP
The plane is made from pastillage icing which dries extremely quickly. If you find it is forming a crust before you have finished making your piece, dampen your hands with a little water.

Couch Potato

The recipient of this fine specimen is sure to realize it is definitely a cake with a message!

CAKE AND DECORATION
25cm (10 in) square cake (page 7) · 1.625kg (3 lb 4 oz) sugarpaste · mauve, blue, brown, egg yellow, green and black food colouring pastes 440g (14 oz) buttercream (page 4) · clear alcohol (gin or vodka) · 280g (9 oz) modelling paste (page 6) · sugar glue (page 6) · brilliant silver lustre powder · brown dusting powder (petal dust/blossom tint) · blue and black food colouring pens

EQUIPMENT
30cm (12 in) oval cakeboard · cocktail sticks (toothpicks) · crimping tool · pieces of foam sponge · fine paintbrush · 2cm (¾ in), 5cm (2 in) and 4cm (1½ in) circle cutters · bone tool · no. 2 and no. 3 piping tubes (tips)

TIP
Store the cake in an airtight container for at least six hours before cutting it into pieces. This will make it easier to work with.

1 Colour 375g (12 oz) sugarpaste pale mauve. Roll out 315g (10 oz) and cover the cakeboard. Make cuts all around the edge using a knife, then apply a crimped line using the crimping tool.

2 Cut the cake into portions as shown in the diagram overleaf. Trim the back piece for the wings and position on the base. Cut the corners from each arm to round off and trim the length to fit the chair. Slice a layer in the cushion cake and lay the pieces side-by-side between each arm. Put the two potato cake

▶ Cut the 25cm (10 in) cake into precise portions as shown.

CUSHION	ARM	CHAIR BASE
POTATO		
POTATO	ARM	CHAIR BACK

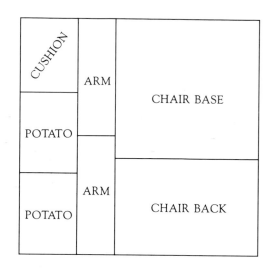

▼ Assemble the five pieces of cake that form the chair. Stick the two potato pieces together and round them off.

pieces together and trim to round off, leaving a bump in the front. Sandwich the cake pieces together with buttercream, then spread a layer over the surface of each cake.

3 In separate bowls, dilute a little blue and mauve food colouring pastes with 1 tsp clear alcohol each. Keeping the foam piece quite dry, 'stipple' the two colours onto the cakeboard. Using a fine paintbrush, paint the crimped line mauve. Put the cakeboard aside to dry.

4 Colour 1kg (2 lb) sugarpaste a blue/mauve colour using blue food colouring paste with a touch of mauve. Using a 60g (2 oz) piece, 'pad' out the arms by rolling a sausage shape for each and positioning along the top outside edge. Smooth the sugarpaste in line with the surface of the cake. 'Pad' each wing to make them fuller.

5 Roll out the remaining blue/mauve sugarpaste and cover the cake. Smooth the sugarpaste around the cushion area and around the arms, cutting away any pleats at the back. Rub any joins closed. Mark the arms with a 2cm (¾ in) circle cutter and add the lines with a knife. Lift the cake and position on the cakeboard. Make a cushion with the remaining pale mauve sugarpaste. Colour 60g (2 oz) sugarpaste bright blue and make another cushion.

6 Colour the remaining sugarpaste potato colour, using equal amounts of brown and egg yellow with a touch of green. Roll our and cover the potato cake, smoothing the sugarpaste around the back. Position the cushions on the chair and press the potato down onto them. Mark the surface to 'wrinkle' the skin. Indent the mouth and eyebrows with the bone tool and the closed eyes with a cocktail stick. Colour 75g (2½ oz) modelling paste potato colour as before. Model the potato's spoon-shaped arms and legs and an oval for the nose, and stick in place.

7 Colour 45g (1½ oz) modelling paste black. Make the remote control and five beer cans. Mark each with the tips of the no. 2 and no 3 piping tubes. Mix 1 tsp clear alcohol with the brilliant silver lustre powder to make a paste. Using a fine paintbrush, paint on the silver details. Stick in place using a little sugar glue.

8 With the remaining modelling paste, make one large plate and two side plates using circle cutters.

Model two cups with handles. Put some potato-colour trimmings into each cup and finely cut a little for the crumbs on the plate. To make the newspaper, roll out and cut four 13 x 7.5cm (5 x 3 in) oblongs and stick in layers on the front of the potato. With the trimmings from the newspaper, roll two thick white hairs and put aside. Leave the cake to dry thoroughly.

9 Dust brown dusting powder over the potato using the fine paintbrush. Dampen the brush a little and paint the brown marks over the skin. It is best to have a real potato close at hand to copy the markings from. Using the blue and black food colouring pens, draw the crosses on the chair, the cup and plate design and the newspaper print. Finally, make two tiny holes in the top of the head and slot in the white hairs.

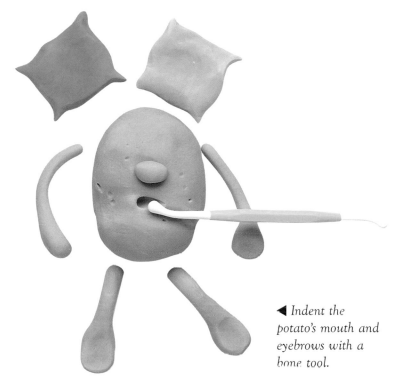

◀ Indent the potato's mouth and eyebrows with a bone tool.

◀ Finely cut up a little of the potato-coloured trimmings to make the crumbs on the plate.

Massage Parlour

This is the cake to choose if you think the man in your life deserves a really special treat!

CAKE AND DECORATION

20cm (8 in) square cake (page 6) · 925g (1 lb 13½ oz) sugarpaste · black, egg yellow, flesh and red food colouring pastes · 250g (8 oz) buttercream (page 4) · clear alcohol (gin or vodka) · 375g (12 oz) modelling paste (page 6) sugar glue (page 6) · 45g (1½ oz) royal icing (page 5) · ½ tsp piping gel · red dusting powder (petal dust/blossom tint) · black and red food colouring pens

EQUIPMENT

28cm (11 in) square cakeboard · ruler · fine paintbrush · cocktail sticks (toothpicks) greaseproof paper piping bag

1 Colour 345g (11 oz) sugarpaste black. Roll out and cover the cakeboard. Indent the lines for the floor tiles using a ruler.

2 Trim the crust from the cake and cut the top flat where it has risen, then cut the cake exactly in half. Sandwich the two cakes together using half the buttercream, then spread a thin layer over the surface of the cake using the remainder. Position the cake on the centre of the cakeboard.

3 Roll out 440g (14 oz) white sugarpaste and cut an oblong measuring 36 x 25cm (14 x 10 in) for the sheet. Trim each corner to round off, then lift carefully and lay over the cake, letting the pleats fall naturally. Reserve 15g (½ oz) white trimmings.

4 Colour the remaining sugarpaste yellow. Thinly roll out and cut an oblong measuring 20 x 15cm (8 x 6 in). Lay over the massage table at an angle.

5 Dilute a little black food colouring paste with a few drops of clear alcohol, then using a fine paintbrush, paint the tiger stripe pattern across the yellow sheet. Set aside to dry.

6 Colour 75g (2½ oz) modelling paste black. Model the pillow with 45g (1½ oz) and position on the bed. Set aside the remainder. Colour 250g (8 oz) modelling paste flesh. Using the photograph as a guide, model the man, positioning on the table as each piece is made. Make his legs first, using a 45g (1½ oz) piece of paste split exactly in half. Roll a ball for his bottom using a 15g (½ oz) piece and position exactly on the centre of the table. For his chest and arms, roll a 45g (1½ oz) ball and flatten slightly. Cut the two arms either side and pinch and pull to shape. Mark his back with a cocktail stick. Position on the table with one arm under the

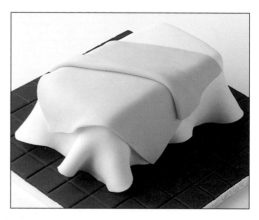

▲ *Lay over the oblong of yellow sugarpaste at an angle, with a fold in the centre.*

▲ *The male and female figures are assembled as shown. The man's bottom is covered with a towel, the* girl wears a black bra, mini skirt and hairband.

▼ *Draw in the girl's lips and other details with a red food colouring pen.*

pillow and other resting on top. Using a 15g (½ oz) piece, roll a tiny ball for his nose and a large ball for his head, marking the grin with a cocktail stick. Using a little sugar glue, secure his head and nose in place.

7 Using the reserved white sugar-paste trimmings, roll out and cut an oblong for a towel and lay over the man's bottom.

8 With 45g (1½ oz) flesh paste cut exactly in half, model the girl's legs and stick in position on the side of the table. With 22g (¾ oz) black modelling paste make her mini-skirt and stick in place on the table just covering the top of her legs. Roll a tiny ball for her nose and a larger ball for her head using 15g (½ oz) flesh paste. Make her chest and arms as before using the remaining flesh paste, sticking firmly in place with her head and nose.

9 With the remaining black paste, make the hairband, a bra strap and roll two balls for the bra. Put the hairband aside, then stick the bra in place. Using white modelling paste, make the three bottles and the jar base, then colour a tiny piece bright red for the jar lid, marking the edge with a cocktail stick. Attach in position.

10 Colour the royal icing cream using a touch of egg yellow. Cut a hole in the tip of the piping bag, fill with the royal icing, then pipe the girl's wavy hair. Position the hairband on her head, then pipe some more wavy hair from the hairband. Pipe the man's hair using a cocktail stick to help shape. Spread the piping gel over the man's back and around the girl's hand for the massage oil.

11 When the cake is completely dry, dust the girl's cheeks with a little red dusting powder. Using the black and red food colouring pens, draw the eyes and eyebrows, the zig-zag pattern on the bottles and the girl's lips.

Breakfast Tray

What better way to say 'Happy Birthday' or 'Be My Valentine' than to present your man with breakfast in bed?

CAKE AND DECORATION

30 x 20cm (12 x 8 in) oblong cake (page 6)
410g (13 oz) buttercream (page 4) · 750g (1½ lb)
sugarpaste · navy blue, red, sage green, pink,
brown and egg yellow food colouring pastes
icing (confectioner's) sugar · 625g (1¼ lb)
modelling paste (page 6) · sugar glue (page 6)
1.5kg (3 lb) pastillage (page 5) · clear alcohol
(gin or vodka) · brilliant silver lustre powder
60g (2 oz) royal icing (page 5)
confectioner's glaze

EQUIPMENT

41 x 30cm (16 x 12 in) oblong cakeboard
cocktail sticks (toothpicks) · flower cutter · small
circle cutter or piping tube (tip) · leaf cutter
fine and medium paintbrushes · sheet of card
tea cup, saucer, plate, knife and fork to use as
moulds · sheet of foil · 6cm (2½ in) circle cutter
heart cutter

1 Cut the top from the cake where it has risen and set aside the trimmings. Cut a layer in the cake and position the two layers side-by-side on the cakeboard. Trim to fit the board, leaving a slight gap all the way round

for the sugarpaste covering. Reserve 22g (¾ oz) buttercream. Spread the remainder over the surface of the cake.

2 Colour the sugarpaste navy blue. To keep the sharp corners, roll out and cut pieces to fit the four sides of the cake first, then cover the top. Colour 375g (12 oz) modelling paste red. Using 90g (3 oz), roll out and cut the thin strips for the top of the tray. Cut out two flowers with the flower cutter. Remove the centres with the small circle cutter. Colour 7g (¼ oz) modelling paste sage green. Using the leaf cutter and the small circle cutter, make four leaves and two flower centres. Stick everything in place using a little sugar glue.

3 Using the sheet of card, make the templates for the tray (see page 79). Colour 1.155kg (2 lb 5 oz) pastillage sage green. Using half, thickly roll out and cut the two handle ends of the tray, one at a time, using the template. When the handle end pieces have formed a firm crust, carefully stick each piece in place. With the remaining sage green pastillage, make the two side pieces using the side template. Stick the two side pieces in place, then dampen the four corners with a little water and rub the join closed.

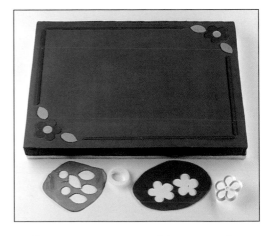

▲ *Decorate two corners of the tray with cut-out flowers and leaves.*

4 Dust the inside of a tea cup with icing sugar. Mould 100g (3½ oz) white modelling paste around the inside of the cup. Keep the paste moving constantly. Trim the top and remove from the tea cup to dry. With the trimmings, model the handle.

5 Dust the plate and saucer with icing sugar. Thinly roll out 130g (4¼ oz) pastillage and lay over the plate. Smooth around the shape of the plate and trim around the edge. Leave to dry supported on the plate. Make the saucer in the same way, using 35g (1¼ oz) pastillage.

6 Using 60g (2 oz) pastillage, roll out half and press the knife into the icing to indent the shape. Cut around the outline and indent the line for the handle. Do the same to make the fork, using the remaining half. Leave to dry on the metal fork for support.

7 Mix 1 tsp clear alcohol with brilliant silver lustre powder to make a paste. Paint a thin coat over the pastillage knife and fork using the fine paintbrush. Leave to dry, then add another thin coat. Stick the handle onto the cup using a little sugar glue.

8 Using the remaining pastillage, cut out the two envelopes, marking the flaps with a knife. Cut out the

▼ *The knife, fork, cup, saucer and plate are easily moulded from household items.*

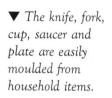

▲ *The bacon rasher is placed on foil to dry while the egg, tomato and sausage are completed. The tomato skin is frilled with a cocktail stick.*

bacon rasher shape. As the icing starts to form a crust, keep moving the rasher to crack the surface and curl up the bacon rind. Crumple a sheet of foil and place the rasher on it to dry.

9 Using the remaining white modelling paste, make the white of the egg and the sausage. Colour 22g (³⁄4 oz) egg yellow and make the egg yolk.

Stick the egg in place on the plate.

10 To make the fried tomatoes, roll a 45g (1½ oz) ball of red modelling paste and cut exactly in half. To make the tomato skin, roll out 15g (½ oz), and cut two circles using the 6cm (2½ in) circle cutter. Frill the edge of each by rolling with a cocktail stick and cover each tomato. Stick onto the plate using a little sugar glue.

11 In separate bowls, dilute a little pink, brown and egg yellow with 1 tsp clear alcohol each. Using the paintbrushes, stipple the colours onto the bacon and sausage and leave to dry. Dilute a little red with 2 tsp clear alcohol. Using the fine paintbrush, paint the red band onto the tea cup, saucer and plate.

12 Crumb the reserved cake crust, and mix with the buttercream to make a ball of truffle paste. Three-quarters fill the pastillage tea cup. Colour royal icing tea colour using a little egg yellow and brown and spoon over the truffle paste, swirling the surface to make it look freshly stirred.

13 When everything is completely dry, put the tea cup, saucer, knife, fork and plate with food onto the tray. Stick the bacon and sausage on the plate using a little sugar glue.

14 Cut out the napkin using the remaining red modelling paste, marking the edge with a knife. Fold up and position on the tray. Cut two hearts from the trimmings using the heart cutter and stick one on each envelope.

15 Using the medium paintbrush and the confectioner's glaze, paint a coat over the tea, cup, saucer, plate and food. Leave to dry, then paint a further coat over the tea and food only. Arrange the envelopes on the tray.

◀ *Confectioner's glaze is painted on to give shine to the tea and food on the plate.*

We are the Champions!

The ideal cake for a football fanatic of any age. Make sure you get the winning team colours right!

CAKE AND DECORATION

20cm (8 in) round cake (page 7) · 1.125kg (2 lb 4 oz) sugarpaste · black, flesh, brown, red, egg yellow and chestnut brown food colouring pastes · 500g (1 lb) buttercream (page 4) · 565g (1 lb 2½ oz) modelling paste (page 6) · sugar glue (page 6) · brilliant silver lustre powder clear alcohol (gin or vodka) · 75g (2½ oz) royal icing (page 5) · black food colouring pen

EQUIPMENT

35cm (12 in) round cakeboard · cocktail sticks (toothpicks) · crimping tool · no. 4 plain piping tube (tip) · polythene bag · fine and medium paintbrushes · 4cm (1½ in), 3cm (1¼ in) and 2.5cm (1 in) circle cutters · 5 greaseproof paper piping bags

---

1 Colour 375g (12 oz) sugarpaste black. Roll out and cover the cakeboard. Using the crimping tool, crimp a border around the edge of the board, then set aside to dry.

2 Cut the top from the cake where it has risen and trim off the crust. Split and fill the cake with half the buttercream, then spread the remainder over the surface of the cake. Roll out 750g (1½ lb) sugarpaste and cover the cake, trimming around the base. Position the cake on the cakeboard, slightly off centre, to leave room for the footballers.

3 Colour 45g (1½ oz) modelling paste black. Split into 22 equal-sized pieces and model all the football boots, using the photograph as a guide. Colour 60g (2 oz) modelling paste pale flesh. Using 45g (1½ oz), roll five balls for the heads and tiny noses for five of the footballers. Mark the smiles with the tip of a no. 4 piping tube. With the remaining piece, model 10 arms and knees. Put all the modelled pieces into a polythene bag to stop them drying out.

4 To make the heads, noses, arms and knees of the remaining six footballers, split 75g (2½ oz) modelling paste into three equal-sized pieces. Colour one piece a darker flesh colour, another light brown and the last piece dark brown. Make two footballers from each colour as before.

5 Colour 90g (3 oz) modelling paste red. Split 30g (1 oz) of the red modelling paste into 22 pieces and model all the football socks. Using 170g (5½ oz) white modelling paste, split into 11 pieces and model the football tops. Roll a ball for each, flatten slightly, then cut the two sleeves either side. Model each top and pinch around the base to hollow out slightly, so each top will fit neatly over the shorts.

6 Split the remaining white modelling paste into 13 equal-sized pieces. Roll a ball with one piece to make the football and set aside. Make all the shorts using 11 of the pieces, marking the lines with a knife. With the remaining piece, roll out and cut the strips for the sock tops. Assemble each footballer, except their heads, resting against the cake using a little sugar glue to stick.

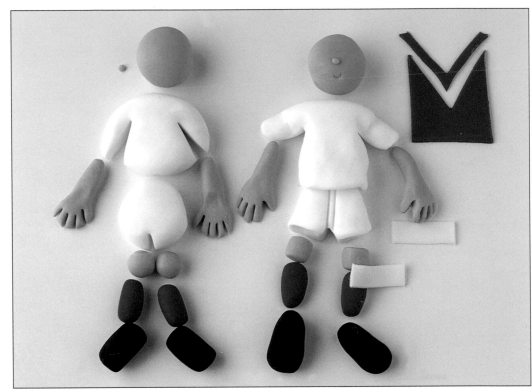

▶ Each footballer is composed of the twelve basic shapes on the left, moulded and shaped into realistic forms as shown on the right.

▼ The championship cup is made from the shapes shown below. Assemble each piece as it is made and place on the cake before painting silver.

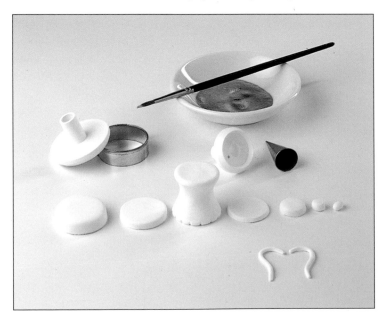

7 Using the remaining red modelling paste, roll out and cut 11 pieces for the front of each football shirt. Cut a 'V' in the top for the stripe. Stick in place with a little sugar glue with the heads on top. Reserve the red modelling paste trimmings.

8 With the remaining piece of white modelling paste, make the championship cup. Using the step photograph as a guide, cut out the base with a 4cm (1½ in) circle cutter, then the next piece with a 3cm (1¼ in) circle cutter. The base of the lid is cut with a 2.5cm (1 in) circle cutter and the end of a piping tube. Reserve the trimmings. Assemble each piece as it is made, sticking them together with a little sugar glue. Position the cup on the centre of the cake.

9 Mix a little brilliant silver lustre powder with clear alcohol. Using the medium paintbrush, paint a thin layer over the cup and on the crimped edge of the cakeboard. Leave to dry for 10 minutes, then paint on another thin coat. Using the red and white modelling paste trimmings, cut the ribbons and lay over the top of each handle.

10 Colour 15g (¼ oz) royal icing cream using a touch of egg yellow. Pipe the hair on two footballers

using a piping bag with a small hole cut in the tip. Colour 22g (³⁄₄ oz) black for three footballers, 22g (³⁄₄ oz) brown for another three footballers, 7g (¹⁄₄ oz) chestnut brown for one and the remainder golden brown using equal amounts of egg yellow and brown for the last two footballers. Pipe the hair as before. Leave the cake to dry before drawing the eyes and eyebrows on each footballer. Remember to vary the facial expressions by altering the slant of the eyebrows and position of the eyes and mouth. Add the markings to the football using the black food colouring pen.

▶ *Use four different shades of royal icing for the footballers' piped hair.*

Decorating Time

The ideal cake for a housewarming party, or perhaps a hint to your other half that the decorating is due?

CAKE AND DECORATION

25cm (10 in) square cake (page 6) · 2.36kg (4 lb 12½ oz) sugarpaste · orange, egg yellow, brown, black and green food colouring pastes 440g (14 oz) buttercream (page 4) · clear alcohol (gin or vodka) · sugar glue (page 6) · 920g (1 lb 13½ oz) modelling paste (page 6) · orange and green food colouring pens · confectioner's glaze · brilliant silver lustre powder · 2 tbsp piping gel · 2-3 tsp icing (confectioner's) sugar

EQUIPMENT

40cm (16 in) square cakeboard · cocktail sticks (toothpicks) · 6cm (2½ in) circle cutter · no. 4 plain piping tube (tip) · plastic glove · pieces of foam sponge · ruler · fine and medium paintbrushes · kitchen roll cardboard tube

1 Colour 625g (1¼ lb) sugarpaste orange. Roll out and cover the cakeboard. Set aside to dry. Cut the top off the cake where it has risen, then cut the cake into four equal strips. Trim the corners to round off, then cut the crust from each end. Using a little buttercream, stick two rolls together end to end, and again, to make two long rolls.

2 Cut 6cm (2½ in) from the end of each roll and with a little buttercream, stick these together to make the border roll. Using the remaining buttercream, spread a thin layer over the surface of each cake.

3 Roll out 75g (2½ oz) white sugarpaste and cut five circles using the 6cm (2½ in) circle cutter. Mark the centre of each with the end of the piping tube and press with your thumb to indent. Stick in place on the ends of each roll, leaving the border roll with just one end covered. Using a cocktail stick, scratch the fine lines.

4 Roll out 675g (1 lb 6 oz) white sugarpaste and place one wallpaper roll down onto it. Trim the sugarpaste at either end, then wrap the sugarpaste around the roll, smoothing the join with your fingers. Repeat for the second wallpaper roll. Cover the border roll in the same way, using the remainder.

5 Dilute a little orange food colouring with 3 tsp clear alcohol. To avoid skin staining, wear a plastic glove. Dip a foam piece into the colour, squeeze out the excess, and keeping the foam quite dry, stipple the pattern over one wallpaper roll.

6 When the stippled roll is dry, position join-side down onto the cakeboard, with the plain white roll resting against it.

▲ *Cut the cake into four equal strips, round off the corners and remove the crust.*

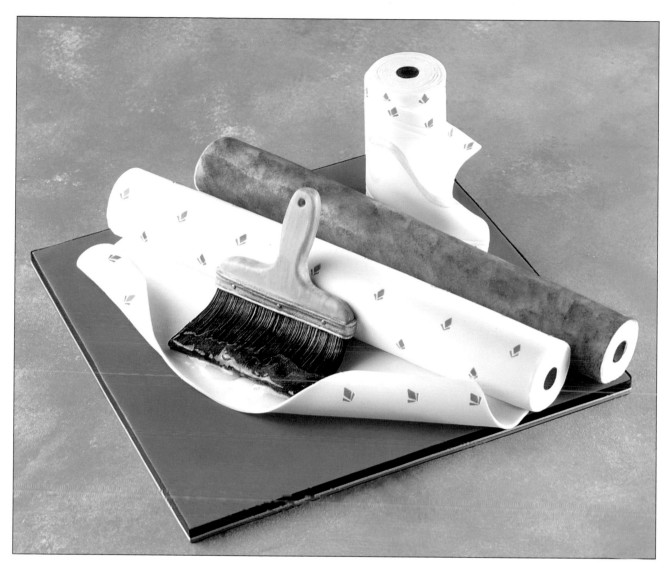

7 Roll out 375g (12 oz) white modelling paste and cut an oblong measuring 46 x 12cm (18 x 4½ in). Position on the board tucked under the white roll. Cut the kitchen roll tube in half and dust with icing sugar. Roll the corners of the sugarpaste over each tube and leave to dry.

8 Roll out 315g (10 oz) white modelling paste and cut a strip measuring 38 x 14cm (15 x 5½ in) for the unrolled piece of the border roll. Using a ruler, indent the lines along the edges. Using a little sugar glue to secure, wrap the sugarpaste around the border roll, leaving the end loose.

9 Colour 75g (2½ oz) modelling paste cream using a touch of egg yellow, and model the paintbrush handle. Push the tip of the no. 4 piping tube into the top to make the hole. Water down a little brown food colouring with a few drops of clear alcohol. Using a medium paintbrush, paint a thin coat over the handle to give a wood effect, then leave to dry thoroughly.

10 Colour 155g (5 oz) modelling paste black. Thickly roll out and cut an oblong for the paste brush slightly smaller in width than the handle. Using a knife, mark lines for the

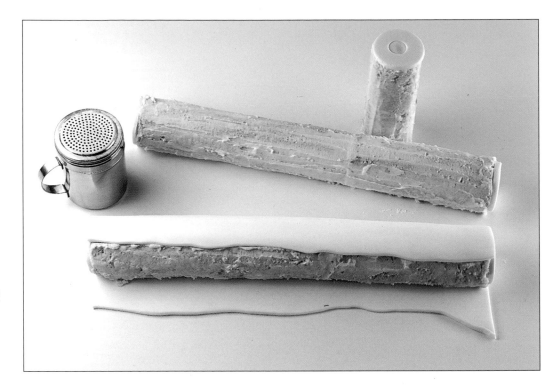

▶ Once the ends have been covered and indented, wrap the sugar-paste around the rolls.

bristles, then position on the unrolled wallpaper curving upwards. With the black trimmings, roll out and cut five circles using the piping tube and stick on the end of each roll.

11 When the curled wallpaper is dry, carefully remove the card-board tubes by twisting them out. Water down a little egg yellow with 2 tsp of clear alcohol. Paint a thin coat over the reverse side of the curled wallpaper and a little onto each end of the stippled roll.

▼ Cut out a black paste oblong slightly narrower than the handle and mark with a knife to resemble bristles.

12 With the orange and green pens, draw the wallpaper pattern on the plain roll and along the edges of the border. Water down a little green food colouring with a few drops of clear alcohol. Using the fine paintbrush, paint scrolls along the centre of the border roll, then position on the cakeboard.

13 Using a little sugar glue, stick the paste brush handle in position. Paint a thin coat of confectioner's glaze over the handle and bristles to give a shine.

14 Roll out the white modelling paste trimmings and cut a strip to fit around the front and sides of the handle. Roll three tiny balls for the pins and stick in place.

15 Mix a little brilliant silver lustre with a few drops of clear alcohol. Using a fine paintbrush, paint a thin coat over the paste brush band, leave to dry, then paint on a further thin coat.

16 To make the paste, mix piping gel with 2-3 tsp of icing sugar and spoon over the bottom of the paste brush.

Rugby Tackle

If you have a real rugby player in mind for this cake, do make him the one who's got the ball!

CAKE AND DECORATION
25cm (10 in) square cake (page 7) · 750g (1½ lb) chocolate buttercream (page 4) · 625g (1¼ lb) sugarpaste · green, flesh, yellow, black, red, egg yellow and chestnut brown food colouring pastes 440g (14 oz) modelling paste (page 6) · sugar glue (page 6) · 45g (1½ oz) royal icing (page 5) black food colouring pen · green, dark green and yellow dusting powders
(petal dust/blossom tint)

EQUIPMENT
25cm (10 in) square cakeboard · cocktail sticks (toothpicks) · large shell or star piping tube (tip) polythene bag · pieces of foam sponge · fine and medium paintbrushes · 3 greaseproof paper piping bags

---

1 Cut the crust from the cake where it has risen and trim the sides. Place the cake on the cakeboard. Set 125g (4 oz) of the chocolate buttercream aside. Using the remainder, fill the gap from the sides of the cake to the edge of the board, then spread a layer over the top of the cake.

2 Colour the sugarpaste green. Roll out and cover the top of the cake.

Using the large star or shell piping tube, repeatedly press into the green sugarpaste, moving in different directions to make the grass effect. Roughly spread the remaining chocolate buttercream over the centre of the grass for the mud.

3 Model the rugby ball from 7g (¼ oz) white modelling paste and stick in place at the front of the cake using a little sugar glue.

4 Colour 125g (4 oz) modelling paste flesh, 100g (3½ oz) yellow, 60g (2 oz) black and 7g (¼ oz) red. Following the photograph, make the four rugby players, two for each side. Make the heads first using 60g (2 oz) flesh modelling paste split into four equal pieces. Mark the open mouths with the end of a paintbrush. As you model each item, place in a polythene bag to prevent drying out. With a further 30g (1 oz) of the flesh paste, make eight arms. With the remaining piece, make eight knees and four noses.

5 Model two yellow rugby tops next, using 45g (1½ oz) for each. With the remaining yellow paste, make four socks. Using 45g (1½ oz) of the white modelling paste for each, make two more rugby tops. With the remainder, model two pairs of shorts and cut four strips for the sock tops.

▲ *Cover the trimmed cake with chocolate buttercream, taking it out to the board edge.*

6 Using the black modelling paste, make two more pairs of shorts, four socks, eight boots, eight strips and two collars. Each collar is cut from the end of a piping tube with a triangular piece then cut from the front. With the red modelling paste, make four strips and two more collars as before.

7 Assemble each rugby player on the cake using a little sugar glue to stick, building up the pile with alternate players. Use pieces of foam for support whilst drying.

8 Colour half the royal icing cream using egg yellow. Snip a hole in the tip of a piping bag and pipe the hair on two rugby players. Split the remaining royal icing in half and colour one half black and the other chestnut brown. Pipe the hair on the other two players as before, using the remaining piping bags. Leave the cake to dry before drawing the eyes and eyebrows on each rugby player using the black food colouring pen. Finally, put a small amount of each colour dusting powder into a dish. With a medium paintbrush, dust the colours onto the grass, letting the powders blend.

▲ *Each rugby player is composed of the same basic shapes. Alternate the team colours for each figure in the pile.*

▼ *When the cake is dry, dust the grass with the three shades of dusting powder.*

51

Squash Court Star

Do you know any sports-mad squash players? If so, this is the perfect cake to stop a really fast mover in his tracks.

CAKE AND DECORATION

25cm (10 in) square cake (page 7) · 1kg (2 lb) sugarpaste · 315g (10 oz) buttercream (page 4) clear alcohol (gin or vodka) · brown, egg yellow, red, dark green, flesh, blue, black and yellow food colouring pastes · 200g (6½ oz) modelling paste (page 6) · sugar glue (page 6) · 30g (1 oz) royal icing (page 5) · blue and black food colouring pens

EQUIPMENT

25cm (10 in) square cake card · 25cm (10 in) square cakeboard · strong non-toxic tape · ruler fine and medium paintbrushes · cocktail sticks (toothpicks) · polythene bag · no. 4 and no. 1 plain piping tubes (tips) · 2 greaseproof paper piping bags · miniature star cutter

1 Stand the cake card on end and tape it to the cakeboard using strong non-toxic tape. Dampen the cake card with a little water. Roll out 280g (9 oz) white sugarpaste and cover the card, trimming around the edge.

2 Trim the top from the cake where it has risen and trim off the crust. Spread a layer of buttercream over the surface of the cake to help the sugarpaste stick and place it on the cakeboard butting up against the upright cake card. Measure the three visible sides of the cake. Using 345g (11 oz) white sugarpaste, roll out and cut pieces to fit. Cover the two sides of the cake first, then the front, keeping the corners sharp.

3 Roll out the remaining white sugarpaste and cover the top of the cake, trimming the edge in line with the sides. Mark floorboard lines across the top of the cake using a ruler as a guide, pressing gently with a knife. Mix clear alcohol with a little brown and egg yellow to make a golden brown colour. Using the medium paintbrush, paint a thin coat over the flooring, moving across the cake following the marked lines. Colour 45g (1½ oz) modelling paste red. Roll out and cut thin strips and stick onto the cake to represent the squash court markings. Reserve the trimmings.

4 Using the photograph overleaf as a guide, model the components needed to make the squash player. As each piece is made, transfer them to a polythene bag to stop them drying out

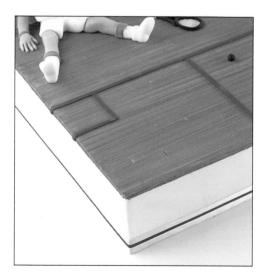

▲ *Keep the corners of the cake sharp to create the right effect.*

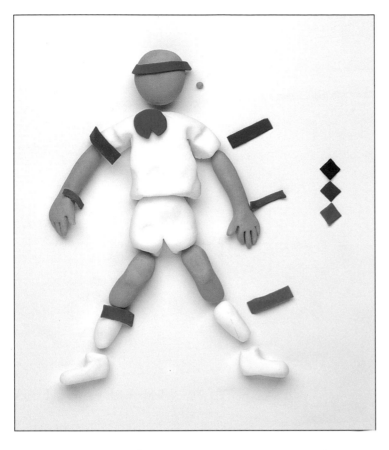

▲ *The squash player is composed of the shapes shown above. The sports kit could be personalized.*

▶ *Three yellow stars and a dazed expression complete the design!*

two eyes, the squash racket handle and cut out a towel. Indent the lines on the towel and racket handle with a knife. Colour the trimmings dark green and make the tiny squash ball.

5 Colour 35g (1¼ oz) modelling paste flesh. Using 15g (½ oz), model a tiny nose and roll a ball for the head. Stick the nose in place and indent the open mouth with the tip of a no. 4 piping tube. Using the remaining flesh-coloured modelling paste, make two arms and legs.

6 Colour 7g (¼ oz) modelling paste blue. Roll out and cut a circle using the end of the piping tube, then cut a small triangle from one side to make the collar. Cut two strips for the sock tops, a headband, two wristbands and a blue diamond shape for the sports top. With the reserved red modelling paste trimmings, cut two strips for the sleeves and another diamond for the sports top motif.

7 Assemble the squash player on the cake, sticking with a little sugar glue. Stick the towel, squash racket handle and ball in place on the court with a little sugar glue.

8 Halve the royal icing and colour one half brown. Using the no. 4 piping tube, pipe on the hair. With white royal icing and the no. 1 piping tube, pipe the netting of the squash racket onto the cake. Colour 7g (¼ oz) modelling paste black. Model the squash racket, positioning the frame over the piped netting. Cut a third diamond for the squash top and stick in place.

9 Colour 7g (¼ oz) modelling paste yellow. Using the miniature star cutter, cut out three stars. Stick in place in an arc just above the squash player's head. Leave the cake to dry thoroughly before drawing the 'crossed' eyes with the blue and black food colouring pens to create a dazed expression.

before being assembled on the cake. Model the sports top first using 30g (1 oz) white modelling paste. With a further 15g (½ oz), model the shorts. Using the remaining white modelling paste, make two socks, two trainers,

Early Morning Call

A perfect cake for any Dad, even one with older children. This happy scene will bring back sweet memories of when they were young.

CAKE AND DECORATION

20cm (8 in) square cake (page 7) · 250g (8 oz) pastillage (page 5) · egg yellow, brown, green, flesh, pink and blue food colouring pastes · 2.25kg (4½ lb) sugarpaste · 220g (7 oz) buttercream (page 4) · clear alcohol (gin or vodka) · sugar glue (page 6) · green and black food colouring pens · 685g (1 lb 6½ oz) modelling paste (page 6) · 75g (2½ oz) royal icing (page 5)· brilliant silver lustre powder

EQUIPMENT

sheet of card · 35cm (14 in) square cakeboard ruler · cocktail sticks (toothpicks) · fine and medium paintbrushes · no. 4 and no. 42 piping tubes (tips) · small ivy leaf cutter · pieces of foam sponge · 2cm (¾ in) and 3cm (1¼ in) plain circle cutters · 2 greaseproof paper piping bags

1 Make the template for the headboard/footboard from card (see page 79). Colour all the pastillage golden brown using egg yellow with a touch of brown. Using the full-sized templates, cut out the centre of the headboard first, then thickly roll out the pastillage and cut the two longer length bed posts. Fold along the dotted lines on the templates to reduce their size and make the centre of the footboard and the two small bed posts. Cut a strip for each centre arch and stick in place, then roll four ball shapes and leave everything to dry on a flat surface.

2 Colour 1kg (2 lb) sugarpaste golden brown. Using 500g (1 lb), roll out and cover the cakeboard. With a ruler, indent lines for the floorboards. Scratch wavy lines along each board using a cocktail stick.

3 Colour 410g (13 oz) sugarpaste green. To make the rug, roll out 170g (5½ oz) and cut out an oblong measuring 25 x 20cm (10 x 8 in). Frill each end with a sharp knife, then mark the lines with a ruler. Position the rug on the cakeboard. With the green trimmings, model the lampshade, marking the pleats with a cocktail stick, and set aside.

4 Slice the top off the cake so it is completely flat and trim off the crust. Cut a strip from the cake measuring 5cm (2 in) in width, then cut this into three, one measuring 7.5cm (3 in) for the blanket chest and two measuring 6cm (2¼ in) for the bedside cabinets. To give extra height, slice a layer in each bedside cabinet and sandwich back together with buttercream. Spread a thin layer of the

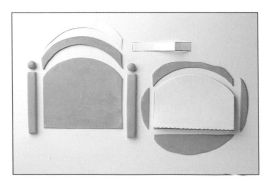

▲ *The pastillage headboard, footboard and bed posts are cut out using the templates.*

remaining buttercream over each cake.

5 Using the remaining golden brown sugarpaste, roll out and cut pieces to fit the two bedside cabinets and the blanket box. Cover the sides first, then the back and front, and finally the top. Make each top slightly larger and round off the front edge by rubbing gently with your thumb. Using the ruler, mark the drawers on the two cabinets. Model the handles with the trimmings.

6 Dilute a little brown food colouring with 5 tsp clear alcohol. Paint a thin coat over the floorboards, headboard and footboard, the bedside cabinets and the blanket box, using the medium paintbrush.

7 Thinly roll out 315g (10 oz) white sugarpaste and cover the bed, then position on the cakeboard. Model the pillows using 45g (1½ oz) each of the white sugarpaste. Pinch around the edge for the frill on two and stick in position in front of the two plain pillows.

8 Draw the ivy trail pattern using the green food colouring pen. Stick the centre of the headboard and footboard in place and the four bedposts with the balls on top. Put the blanket box on the cakeboard and push it up against the footboard to hold it in place.

▼ *Level off the cake and cut it into pieces as described in Step 4.*

▶ *Mum and Dad's bodies only need to be basic shapes as they are hidden by the bedclothes.*

9 Colour 260g (8½ oz) modelling paste flesh. Roll 45g (1½ oz) into a sausage, flatten slightly and place on the bed for Mum's body. Cut a 22g (¾ oz) piece in half and roll two thin sausages for Dad's legs and position on the bed. Roll a ball with 22g (¾ oz) and stick to the pillow for Mum's head. Mark her mouth with the tip of the no. 4 piping tube. With a 15g (½ oz) piece, model her arm and stick in position. Using a 75g (2½ oz) piece, roll a ball and flatten slightly. Cut two arms either side and model Dad's chest and arms, marking the details with a cocktail stick. Stick in place resting against the pillow.

10 To make the green sheet, thinly roll out the remaining green sugarpaste and cut an oblong measuring 25 x 18cm (10 x 7 in). Arrange on the bed, folding back under Mum's chin.

11 Roll out 345g (11 oz) white sugarpaste and cut an oblong measuring 25 x 15cm (10 x 6 in). Using the small ivy leaf cutter, cut out the pattern on the cover. Lift gently and lay the cover on top of the green sheet,

then fold the top of the sheet over. Put Dad's hands in position.

12 With 75g (2½ oz) white modelling paste, model the lamp base then roll out and cut the cloths, marking the edging pattern with the tip of the no. 4 piping tube. Stick the cloths in place then stick the lamp base in position with the lampshade on top. Place the lampshade cloth on top and smooth down.

13 Colour 125g (4 oz) modelling paste pale mauve using equal amounts of pink and blue food colouring paste. Model the girl's nightie using a 60g (2 oz) piece, and position as shown. With the remaining piece, model the dressing gown, reserving the trimmings. Colour 45g (1½ oz) modelling paste pale pink. Using 7g (¼ oz), make Mum's slippers. With the remaining piece, model the baby's nightie and stick in position.

14 Colour 75g (2½ oz) modelling paste dark blue. Roll a sausage with a 45g (1½ oz) piece and cut down the centre leaving 2cm (¾ in) at the top for the boy's pyjama bottoms. Model into a sitting position and stick on the side of the bed. With the remaining piece, make the breakfast tray. Mark the two lines either side then cut out the handles using the tip of the no. 4 piping tube. Position on the bed using pieces of foam to support the sides until dry.

15 Model the boy's pyjama top from a 30g (1 oz) piece of white modelling paste. Trim the neckline with the dark blue trimmings, model a tiny flattened ball shape for the baby's hairband and roll two tiny balls for the slipper trims.

16 With the remaining white modelling paste, make the card, newspaper, clock, spoon, egg cup and cup. Make the saucer and plate using the circle cutters, and the piece of toast. With the white, blue and pale mauve trimmings, make the present.

17 Using the remaining flesh paste, model the heads, noses, hands, feet, the egg and the toast crust.

Dad's head is made from a 22g (³/4 oz) piece, the children's from two pieces each weighing 15g (¹/2 oz) and the baby's 7g (¹/4 oz). Mark the mouths using a cocktail stick and the no. 4 piping tube.

18 Split the royal icing in half. Colour half cream using a touch of egg yellow and half brown. Using the no. 42 piping tube and the cream icing, pipe hair for Dad, the boy and baby. Position the hairband on the baby's head and pipe a pony tail. With the no. 42 piping tube and the brown icing, pipe hair for Mum and the little girl, and the spilt tea. Use a cocktail stick to apply the tea drips on the egg cup.

19 Mix a little brilliant silver lustre powder with clear alcohol. Using a fine paintbrush, paint the clock, the spoon and the card design.

20 Using the black food colouring pen, draw the eyes, the clock face and the newspaper. With just a touch of egg yellow, paint the top of the toast for the butter.

▼ *The charm of this cake lies in its attention to detail; each of the characters has a distinct personality.*

All Too Much

Recognize this family scene? Present a long-suffering Grandad with this comical get together and he's sure to see the joke!

CAKE AND DECORATION

25cm (10 in) square cake (page 7) · 1.75kg (3½ lb) sugarpaste · egg yellow, brown, black, flesh, blue, red, mauve, green, yellow and chestnut food colouring pastes · 500g (1 lb) buttercream (page 4) · sugar glue (page 6) 575g (1 lb 3½ oz) modelling paste (page 6) clear alcohol (gin or vodka) · brilliant silver lustre powder · 60g (2 oz) royal icing (page 5) · black food colouring pen

EQUIPMENT

36cm (14 in) oval cakeboard · cocktail sticks (toothpicks) · fine paintbrush · 6cm (2½ in) and 2.5cm (1 in) circle cutters · pieces of foam sponge no. 4 piping tube (tip) · blossom cutter 4 greaseproof paper piping bags

---

1 Colour 625g (1¼ lb) sugarpaste dark yellow using egg yellow food colouring paste with a touch of brown added. Roll out 375g (12 oz) of the sugarpaste and cover the cakeboard. Reserve the trimmings. Indent the pattern around the edge of the cakeboard with the tail-end of a paintbrush and set aside to dry.

2 Cut the cake as shown in the diagram. Trim the top of the sofa back and round off the edges. Position on the sofa base. Trim each arm to round off and position one at either end of the sofa. Cut an even layer in the seat cushion cake to make two, and trim the centre of each to make a dip. Cut the two circular cakes using a 6cm (2½ in) circle cutter. Cut a layer in each to make four circular cakes and discard one.

3 To make the table, sandwich the the three circles together with a little buttercream. Sandwich the sofa cake pieces together except for the seat cushions, and spread a layer of buttercream over both cakes and the two seat cushions.

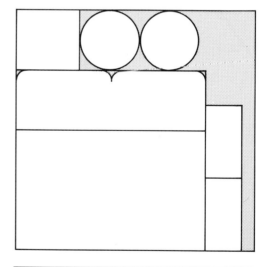

▲ *Cut the cake as shown in the diagram. Assemble to make the sofa and table.*

4 Colour 1.125kg (2 lb 4 oz) sugar-paste cream, using a touch of egg yellow. With a 30g (1 oz) piece, roll two sausage shapes and pad out each arm along the top outside edge. Smooth the sugarpaste in line with the surface of the cake. Knead the dark yellow trimmings from the cakeboard covering and 1kg (2 lb) of the cream sugarpaste together until streaky. Roll out and cover the sofa, smoothing the sugar-paste around the shape. With the trimmings, roll out and cover each seat cushion and put in place on the sofa. Mark the lines on the sofa with a knife. Lift the sofa and position on the cakeboard.

5 Roll out 155g (5 oz) dark yellow sugarpaste and cut a circle for the tablecloth. Mark the pattern around the

edge as before. Lay over the table, encouraging the pleats. Position on the cakeboard, pushed up against the end of the sofa. Split the remaining dark yellow paste into two equal pieces and make two cushions. Stick one at either end of the sofa using a little sugar glue. Model two more cushions using the remaining cream sugarpaste and roll out and cut the square tablecloth, marking the pattern around the edge as before. Stick in place using a little sugar glue.

6 Colour 100g (3½ oz) modelling paste black. With 75g (2½ oz), make the man's trousers. Model the boy's trousers and the girl's shoes from the remainder. Put the shoes aside, then stick both trousers in place.

7 Make the man's top from 60g (2 oz) white modelling paste. Press onto the top of the trousers and arrange the arms. Colour 90g (3 oz) modelling paste flesh. Using 22g (¾ oz) roll a ball for the man's head and nose. Make his feet and hands using 15g (½ oz) and stick in place. Mark his open mouth with the tip of a no. 4 piping tube.

8 Colour 100g (3½ oz) modelling paste blue. To make the girl and the climbing baby, first model the leggings for the girl from 30g (1 oz), then make the baby's romper using a further 30g (1 oz) piece. Model the girl's top with 22g (¾ oz) white modelling paste. Using 30g (1 oz) of the flesh modelling paste, make the two heads, two noses and four hands. Mark their smiles with a cocktail stick. Roll out 7g (¼ oz) blue paste and cut out two flowers using the blossom cutter. Cut out the centre of one and stick on the girl's top. Cut the other in half for the collar. Support the baby and girl on the cake with foam pieces whilst drying.

▶ *The climbing baby and the girl are made together using blue modelling paste. A blossom cutter is used to decorate the girl's top.*

9 Colour 75g (2½ oz) modelling paste red. Using a 45g (1½ oz) piece, model the golf bag and stick in place, resting against the sofa. Colour 30g (1 oz) modelling paste pale mauve and 30g (1 oz) mauve. Make the boy's top using 22g (¾ oz) of the paler colour and make the blonde baby's romper and a hairband with the mauve. Using 30g (1 oz) flesh modelling paste, make two heads, two noses and four hands. Mark their open mouths using the tip of a no. 4 piping tube. Stick in place using pieces of foam for support whilst drying.

10 With the remaining white modelling paste, make the cup with a handle, the saucer using a 2.5cm (1 in) circle cutter, the boy's shoes, two quarters cut from a ball of paste for the red and white ball, the golf bag pocket, straps and side design, and four golf club heads. Bend a cocktail stick until it breaks slightly. Stick each golf club head on a cocktail stick and put aside to dry.

11 With the remaining red paste, complete the red and white ball, make the skipping rope handles and cut some building bricks. Place one under the climbing baby's hand.

12 With the remaining flesh modelling paste, roll a long sausage for the skipping rope and indent with a cocktail stick. Wrap around the blonde baby and stick in place with the handles.

13 With the remaining blue modelling paste, make two hairbands for the girl and one for the blonde baby. Cut more building bricks. Knead the remaining pale mauve modelling paste with a little blue until streaky and make another ball.

14 Colour 7g (¼ oz) modelling paste pale brown and make the teddy. Using a little sugar glue, stick in position on the sofa. Using the green

and yellow food colouring pastes, colour 22g (¾ oz) modelling paste for each. Make the remaining building bricks. Arrange all the bricks around the cake, sticking in place.

15 Mix 1 tsp clear alcohol with brilliant silver lustre powder and paint the golf clubs. Colour 15g (½ oz) royal icing grey. Using a piping bag without a tube, snip a hole in the tip and pipe the man's wavy hair. Colour another 15g (½ oz) cream and pipe the hair on the boy and baby. Put a blue hairband on top of the baby's head and pipe more hair for the top knot. Colour the remaining royal icing chestnut and pipe the hair bunches for the girl and top knot for the climbing baby, adding the hairbands made earlier.

16 Mix the remaining royal icing together to make coffee colour. Water it down slightly and fill the cup, letting the icing run down the tablecloth for the spilt drink. Push three golf clubs into the top of the golf bag and position the broken club in the boy's hands. Leave the cake to dry thoroughly before drawing the eyes and eyebrows on all the characters, and the eyes and nose on the teddy with the black food colouring pen.

▲ *Make the teddy and skipping rope as shown. The building bricks are made by cutting the paste into even-sized cubes.*

All Jogged Out

Not quite as fit as he wants to be? Treat him to this cake and it's sure to provide the energy for one more try.

CAKE AND DECORATION

25cm (10 in) round cake (page 7) · 440g (14 oz) buttercream (page 4) · 1.25kg (2½ lb) sugarpaste black, green, egg yellow, brown, navy blue, flesh, red and chestnut brown food colouring pastes · 315g (10 oz) modelling paste (page 6) clear alcohol (gin or vodka) · sugar glue (page 6) 30g (1 oz) royal icing (page 5) · black food colouring pen · red dusting powder (petal dust/blossom tint)

EQUIPMENT

36cm (14 in) oval cakeboard · cocktail sticks (toothpicks) · large shell or star piping tube (tip) fine and medium paintbrushes no. 4 and no. 2 plain piping tubes (tips) plastic dowelling rod

1 Cut the crust from the top of the cake following where it has risen. Cut the cake as shown with a winding path through the centre. Use the trimmings to build up the height at the back of the cake. Position the cake on the cakeboard and place the piece of cake cut from the front on the cakeboard to one side at the back.

Sandwich the trimmed cake pieces together with buttercream, then spread a layer over the surface of the cake.

2 Colour 375g (12 oz) sugarpaste grey using black food colouring paste. Roll out 155g (5 oz), cut a strip for the winding path and position over the top of the cake. With the remainder, roll out and cover the front of the board, pushing the sugarpaste up the sides of the cake to make the path at the front. Rub the join closed.

3 Colour 875g (1¾ lb) sugarpaste green. Roll out and cut into two pieces, one slightly larger than the other. Position the pieces either side of the winding path with the larger piece at the back. Using the large shell or star piping tube, push the tip repeatedly into the green sugarpaste to make the textured grass effect.

▲ *Cut the cake into a rough mound shape, with a winding path through the centre.*

▲ *The grass effect is made by pushing the tip of a piping tube into the sugarpaste.*

4 To make the park bench, roll 200g (6½ oz) white modelling paste into a thick sausage and cut out the front to make the seat. Mark the lines for the woodgrain with a knife. Using the modelling paste that was cut away from the seat, make the litter bin, again marking the wood lines with a knife, and model the three birds.

5 In separate bowls, dilute a little egg yellow and brown with 1 tsp clear alcohol each. Using a paintbrush,

paint a little of each colour onto the seat of the park bench, then use brown for the edges and to highlight the grain at either end. Paint the wood effect onto the litter bin and stipple a little of each colour onto the birds. Paint the top of the litter bin and the beak of each bird yellow. When dry, position on the cake.

6 Colour 30g (1 oz) modelling paste navy blue. Using the photograph as a guide, make the jog top, marking

▲ *The rabbit is made from nine basic shapes, with markings and white detail added later.*

down the centre and around the edge of each cuff with a knife. Reserve the trimmings. Model the shorts, socks and trainers using 22g (¾ oz) white modelling paste. Colour 30g (1 oz) flesh and make the head, marking the open mouth with the tip of a no. 4 piping tube, a nose, two hands, two legs and the bunny. Stick everything in position on the cake.

7 Using the navy blue trimmings, cut strips for the shorts and sock tops and stick in place. Cut out a small square for a piece of rubbish. With the remaining white modelling paste, make the newspaper, the rubbish, the chest, tail, cheeks and mouth of the bunny, marking the open mouth with the tip of a no. 2 piping tube, and roll out and cut strips for the jog clothes, litter bin and grass sign. Make the signpost by cutting two small strips and stick each in place on top of the plastic dowelling rod. Model the balls for the top and stick in place. Using the red food colouring paste, colour 7g (¼ oz) and cut the red strips for the jog clothes.

8 Colour the royal icing chestnut brown. Using a no. 4 piping tube, pipe the jogger's hair, then put the cake aside to dry. Using the black food colouring pen, draw the eyes on the jogger, birds and bunny. Draw the lettering on the newspaper and signs. Give the jogger flushed cheeks with red dusting powder. Push the signpost into the cake.

▶ *The jogger is composed of the twelve basic shapes on the left, moulded and shaped into realistic forms as shown on the right.*

Bathroom Sink

The perfect cake for a man approaching middle-age who can take a joke – or perhaps a hint to tidy the mess that he always leaves behind?

CAKE AND DECORATION

25cm (10 in) square cake (page 7) · 1.28kg (2 lb 9 oz) sugarpaste · black, chestnut brown, red and blue food colouring pastes · 625g (1¼ lb) buttercream (page 4) · 75g (2½ oz) pastillage (page 5) · clear alcohol (gin or vodka) · sugar glue (page 6) · 315g (10 oz) modelling paste (page 6) · brilliant silver lustre powder · black and red food colouring pens · 3-4 tsp piping gel

EQUIPMENT

25cm (10 in) square cakeboard · ruler · miniature square cutter · cocktail sticks (toothpicks) · sheet of card · fine and medium paintbrushes · shell piping tube (tip)

---

1 Roll out 315g (10 oz) sugarpaste and cover the cakeboard. Using a ruler, indent lines for the tiles, 3cm (1¼ in) apart. Colour the sugarpaste trimmings black. On each tile corner, cut out a small square using the miniature square cutter, then replace with squares cut from black sugarpaste.

2 Cut the top from the cake where it has risen and trim off the crust. Cut the cake into four equal pieces and sandwich one on top of the other using three-quarters of the buttercream.

3 Cut out the sink from the top layer only. Keep your knife at an inward angle to form the sloping sides of the basin and cut a straight line at the back for the taps.

4 Cut out a strip from the base of the cake at the front, 2cm (¾ in) in height and depth. Spread the remaining buttercream over the surface of the cake. Colour 750g (1½ lb) sugarpaste pale chestnut brown. Cover the back of the cake first by placing the cake on the rolled out sugarpaste and cutting around it. Cover the two sides in the same way, then cut a strip for the base at the front of the cake.

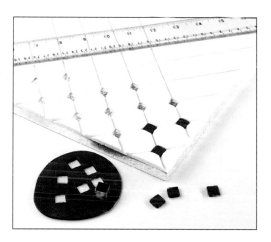

▲ *A black tile occupies the space left when the corners of four white tiles are removed.*

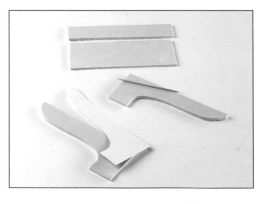

▲ *The sink back, sides and shelf are cut from pastillage with the aid of a template.*

5 Position the cake on the cake-board. With the remaining pale chestnut paste, roll out and cut a piece to fit the front of the cake. Indent the drawer and cupboard with a ruler and use a knife to mark the panels. With a cocktail stick, mark the lines for the woodgrain.

6 Make the templates for the sink frame using the sheet of card (see page 79). Colour the pastillage pale chestnut brown. Using the templates, roll out and cut the pieces for the sink frame. Mark the woodgrain using a cocktail stick, before the icing forms a crust. With the pastillage trimmings, model the two ends of the towel rail. Leave everything to dry on a completely flat surface.

7 Dilute a little chestnut brown food colouring paste with 1 tbsp clear alcohol. Using the medium paintbrush, paint a colour wash over the cabinet and sink frame to highlight the woodgrain.

8 Using 155g (5 oz) white sugarpaste, roll out and cut the square tiles. Stick in place on the pastillage piece for the back of the sink frame and cover the top of the cake, leaving a space around the edge for the two side frame pieces when assembled.

▼ *The pots, tube, taps and flannel are made as shown and marked with a knife. Fold the flannel roughly before positioning on the sink.*

9 Using the remaining white sugarpaste, thinly roll a sausage for the sink rim and stick in place with a little sugar glue. Roll out and cut a piece to fit the basin, smoothing around the rim. Indent the overflow with the tip of a shell piping tube and the plug hole rim with the opposite end.

10 Colour 200g (6½ oz) modelling paste red. Roll out and cut the two towels, indenting the lines at either end with a knife. Place one crumpled on the floor and fold the other and stick in place on the side of the cabinet. Stick the two towel rail ends in place. With the trimmings, make the two flannels, again indenting the pattern with a knife, and the toothbrush handle.

11 Using white modelling paste, make the two taps, a pair of boxer shorts, the denture pot, a bar of soap, the toothpaste tube with the paste squeezed out, the wrinkle cream pot, the hair restorer, the razor, the bristles for the toothbrush and the knobs for the cabinet. Colour 7g (¼ oz) modelling paste black, then make the razor end, the plug and the lid for the hair restorer. Colour 15g (½ oz) modelling paste grey and model the two socks.

12 When the sink frame is completely dry, stick in place using a little sugar glue. Mix some brilliant silver lustre powder with clear alcohol. Using a fine paintbrush, paint a thin coat over the taps and towel rail, leave to dry, then repeat.

13 Colour a tiny amount of trimmings pale blue and stick a dot onto the cold tap. Do the same for the hot tap, using red. With the black and red pens, draw the pattern on the cabinet knobs, the hearts on the boxer shorts and the names on the bottle and pots. Stick everything in place. Finally, spoon piping gel into the basin for the water and put a tiny 'drip' on the end of the tap.

Monkey Business

Give this cake to your hairy hunk and he's sure to go bananas!

CAKE AND DECORATION

1 x 2ltr (4 pint), 1 x ¾ltr (1¼ pint) and 2 x 150ml (¼ pint) bowl-shaped cakes (page 7) · 1.5kg (3 lb) sugarpaste · green, black, brown, egg yellow and yellow food colouring pastes · 500g (1 lb) buttercream (page 4) · sugar glue (page 6) · 60g (2 oz) modelling paste (page 6) · clear alcohol (gin or vodka)

EQUIPMENT

28cm (11 in) petal-shaped cakeboard · cocktail sticks (toothpicks) · fine paintbrush

---

1 Colour 250g (8 oz) sugarpaste green. Roll out and cover the cakeboard. Mark on the criss-cross lines with the back of a knife, then set aside to dry. Slice the tops off the cakes where they have risen, leaving a rounded edge. Trim off the crusts.

2 To make the gorilla's face, cut a curve in the front of the medium-sized bowl cake to shape the nose and mouth area. Trim from the top down to the curve to make room for the eyes. Cut a slight dip at the back of the head.

3 For the gorilla's arms, make two cuts either side of the large bowl

cake 4cm (1½ in) apart. Trim the front and back of the cake round to each arm and round off the edges. For the legs, trim one side of each small bowl cake, so they will sit against the body.

4 Slice a layer in the head and body and sandwich back together using half the buttercream. Position the cake on the cakeboard and stick the head and legs in place with a little buttercream. With the remainder, spread a layer over the cake surface.

5 Colour 250g (8 oz) sugarpaste brown. Pad out the nose area with a 30g (1 oz) piece, then thickly roll out 100g (3½ oz) and cover the face completely, cutting a fat, uneven, number eight shape. Indent the eye area and mark all the lines with a knife. Reserve the trimmings for the ears. With the remaining brown sugarpaste, split into four equal-sized pieces and model the hands and feet, again marking the fur lines with a knife. Set aside to dry.

6 Colour 7g (¼ oz) sugarpaste golden brown using equal amounts of brown and egg yellow. Model the nose and roll a thin sausage for the mouth and stick in place using a little sugar glue. Mark the lines on the nose with a knife.

▲ *Carve arms and a muzzle on the two large cakes. The small cakes form the legs.*

▲ *Mark the fur lines with a scalpel. Try to create a natural look.*

7 Model the whites of the gorilla's eyes and make two small dots for the centre of each using a little white sugarpaste. Colour the remaining sugarpaste very dark brown using equal quantities of black and brown. Model two brown irises and assemble each eye in position on the face.

8 Pad the top of the gorilla's head with 22g (¾ oz) dark brown sugarpaste to make it slightly pointed.

Roll out 250g (8 oz) dark brown sugarpaste and cover the head. Smooth the sugarpaste around the face and mark the fur lines with a knife. With a 15g (½ oz) piece, make the ears using the brown trimmings for the centres and stick in place. Mark the fur lines.

9 Roll out the remaining dark brown sugarpaste and cover the gorilla's body from the front, smoothing under the head and round to the back. Smooth the joins closed at the neck and back by rubbing in a circular motion. Outline the top of the legs and around each arm with the back of a knife. Stick the hands and feet in position. Mark the fur lines as before.

10 Split the yellow modelling paste into three equal-sized pieces. Using the photograph below as a guide, make the three bananas. Dilute a little each of the black, brown, green and egg yellow food colouring paste with clear alcohol. Paint the detail onto each banana. When dry, stick in position.

▶ *Make three banana skins by splitting a fat sausage of paste into a four-pointed star. Paint with black, brown, green and yellow markings.*

72

Chaos in the Kitchen

*The perfect cake for any would-be chef.
Thankfully the mess will disappear
when he starts to nibble the evidence!*

CAKE AND DECORATION

20cm (8 in) square cake (page 7) · 1.25kg (2½ lb)
sugarpaste · egg yellow, brown, black, blue, flesh,
sage green, orange and red food colouring pastes
625g (1¼ lb) buttercream (page 4) · 650g
(1 lb 6 oz) modelling paste (page 6) · clear alcohol
(gin or vodka) · sugar glue (page 6) · brilliant
silver lustre powder · black food colouring pen

EQUIPMENT

30cm (12 in) square cakeboard · cocktail sticks
(toothpicks) · ruler · fine and medium
paintbrushes · shell piping tube (tip) · no. 1
piping tube (tip) · 2cm (¾ in), 2.5cm (1 in), 4cm
(1½ in) and miniature circle cutters · piece of
voile netting · crimping tool
lined rolling pin

1 Colour 500g (1 lb) sugarpaste golden brown using a little egg yellow and brown. Roll out 345g (11 oz) and cover the cakeboard. Using a ruler, indent the lines for the floor tiles. Dilute a little of the same colours with 1 tbsp clear alcohol. Paint a colour wash over the floor tiles using a medium paintbrush.

2 Slice the top from the cake where it has risen and trim off the crust. Cut the cake into three strips, then cut a layer in each strip. Using half the buttercream, sandwich the layers together using the photograph as a guide. Position the cake on the cakeboard. Spread the remaining buttercream over the surface of the cake.

3 Roll out 750g (1½ lb) sugarpaste and cut pieces to fit the sides of the cake. Cover the back, then the front, and finally the two ends. Reserve the trimmings. Using a knife, mark the lines for the doors, drawers and panelling on the cabinets, and the cooker and washing machine. Indent the knobs with the tip of a shell piping tube and the buttons with a no. 1 piping tube.

4 Roll out the remaining golden brown sugarpaste and cover the top of the cake for the work surface. Cut away the sugarpaste above the cooker and replace with a piece made from the white trimmings to make the hob. Mark the air vent on top using a knife.

5 To make room for the sink, cut out a 4cm (1½ in) square from the work surface, removing just the sugarpaste. Roll out 30g (1 oz) white modelling paste and cut an oblong for

▲ *Cut and layer the cake with buttercream.
Assemble the pieces into an L shape.*

73

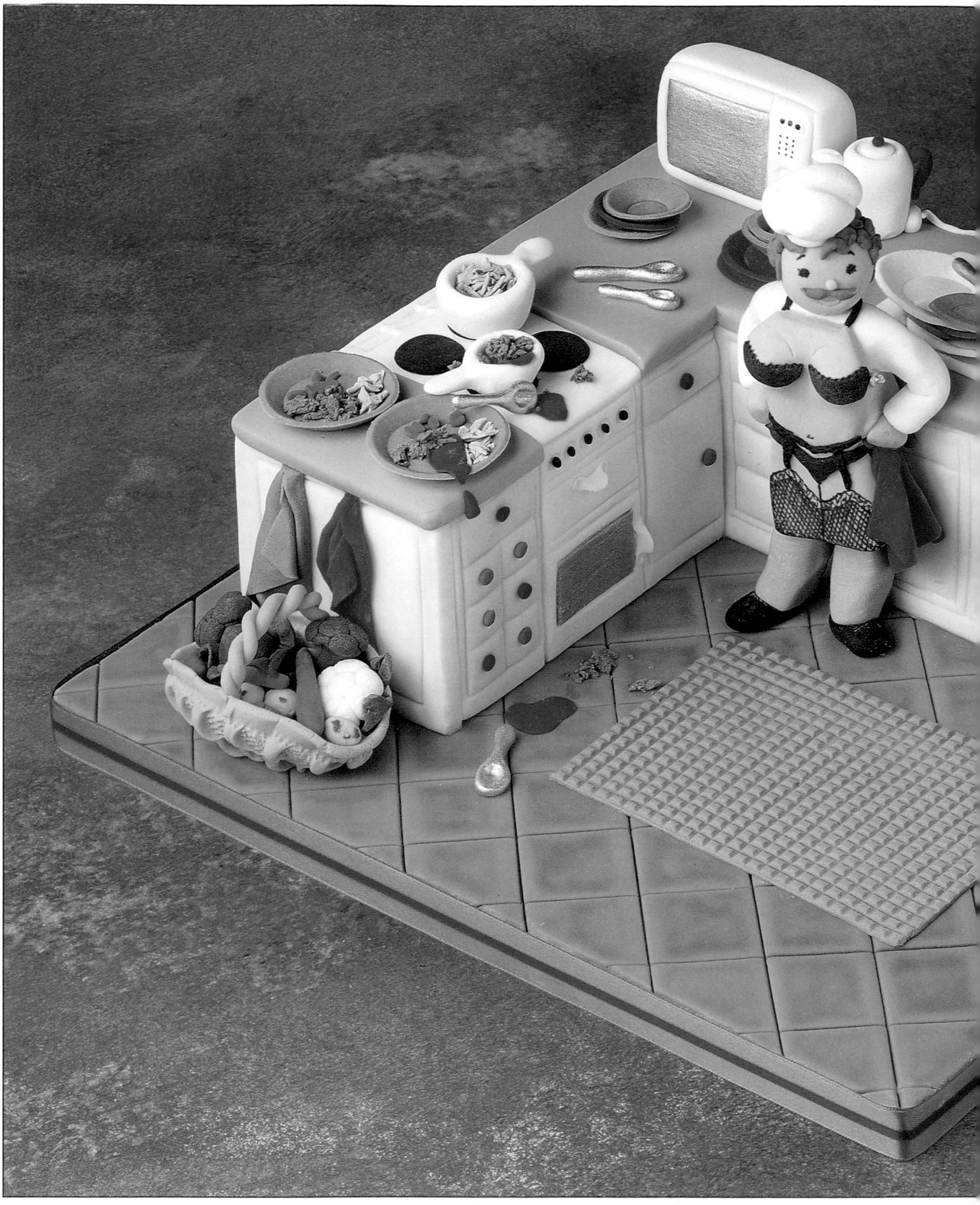

the sink measuring 5 x 8cm (2 x 3½ in). Press down in place and mark the draining board with the end of a paintbrush. Dilute a little egg yellow with 1 tbsp clear alcohol. Using the medium paintbrush, paint a colour wash over the kitchen cabinets.

6 To make the man, first colour 22g (¾ oz) modelling paste black. Using a 7g (¼ oz) piece, model two shoes. Colour 45g (1½ oz) pale blue and make his trousers. Using 60g (2 oz) white modelling paste, model the chef's hat and his top. Colour 100g (3½ oz) flesh. Using 15g (½ oz), roll a ball for his head, make a nose and two hands. Mark his smile with a cocktail stick. Assemble on the cake supported by the cabinets, and stick in place using a little sugar glue.

7 Using 30g (1 oz) flesh modelling paste, model the saucy apron with blown-up boobs. Make the apron underwear and strap using 7g (¼ oz) black modelling paste. Stick the

▼ *The man and his chef's hat are composed of the basic shapes on the left, moulded and shaped into the realistic forms on the right.*

▲ *The apron is made from flesh modelling paste. The black underwear is stuck on top, then frilled with a cocktail stick.*

underwear in place on the apron. 'Frill' the suspender and bra edge by pressing in with the tip of a cocktail stick, then using a little sugar glue, stick in place with the apron strap around the man's neck.

8 With the remaining black modelling paste, roll out and cut four circles for the hob using a 2cm (¾ in) circle cutter. With the trimmings, make five oven controls. Stick in place using a little sugar glue.

9 With the remaining white paste, make the microwave with 75g (2½ oz), then make the kettle, saucepans, taps, spoons, cooker handles, washing machine door using the 4cm (1½ in) and 2.5cm (1 in) circle cutters, the plates, and the white of the cauliflower, pressing the top with the piece of voile net to mark the pattern. Make the tiny blow tube for the apron.

10 Using 45g (1½ oz) flesh modelling paste, make the vegetable basket with its twisted handle. Crimp around the top edge and at the side using the crimping tool. With the remainder, make the potatoes.

11 Colour 22g (¾ oz) modelling paste dark green. Using the photograph as a guide, make the broccoli, cauliflower leaves and a cabbage. Stick the leaves to the underside of the cauliflower. Colour 7g (¼ oz) orange. Model the carrots, then arrange everything in thc basket. Chop up a little of the orange modelling paste to make the cooked carrot for the plates and set aside. Stick the basket handle in place.

▶ *Mark the vegetable basket with a crimping tool. Model the vegetables, marking the cauliflower and broccoli with a piece of net.*

12 Colour 100g (3½ oz) modelling paste sage green. Roll out 60g (2 oz), then roll the lined rolling pin over the paste to indent small squares. Cut out the kitchen mat and stick in place with a little sugar glue. With the remaining sage green modelling paste, make the plates, bowls, tea towels, cup and cup hook. Chop some up for the cooked vegetable and make some cabinet knobs. Stick a tiny piece onto the washing machine door.

13 Colour 45g (1½ oz) bright blue. Make some more plates, tea towels, cabinet knobs and another cup and cup hook. Stick a piece of bright blue paste onto the washing machine door.

14 Colour 45g (1½ oz) modelling paste red. Make the spilled sauce, the kettle handle and knob, more plates, tea towels, cabinet knobs and the last cup and cup hook. Stick a small piece on the washing machine door. Indent the centre of the door using the miniature circle cutter. Stick everything in place using a little sugar glue.

15 Colour 22g (¾ oz) modelling paste brown. Stick little pieces over the man's head to make his hair and on his face for the moustache. Chop some up for the meat, sticking

some on the floor, plates, cooker and in the saucepan. Stick a little onto each potato.

16 Mix 1 tsp clear alcohol with brilliant silver lustre powder. Using the fine paintbrush, paint a coat over the cooker door, microwave door, taps, spoons and apron blow tube. Leave to dry, then paint on another coat. Paint a little over the washing machine door. Leave the cake to dry thoroughly before drawing on the man's eyes and eyebrows using the black food colouring pen. Draw the apron stockings and navel and the microwave and washing machine buttons.

▲ *Make plates in various sizes and colours using the circle cutters.*

▼ *Arrange all the vegetables and crockery for an attractive yet chaotic effect!*

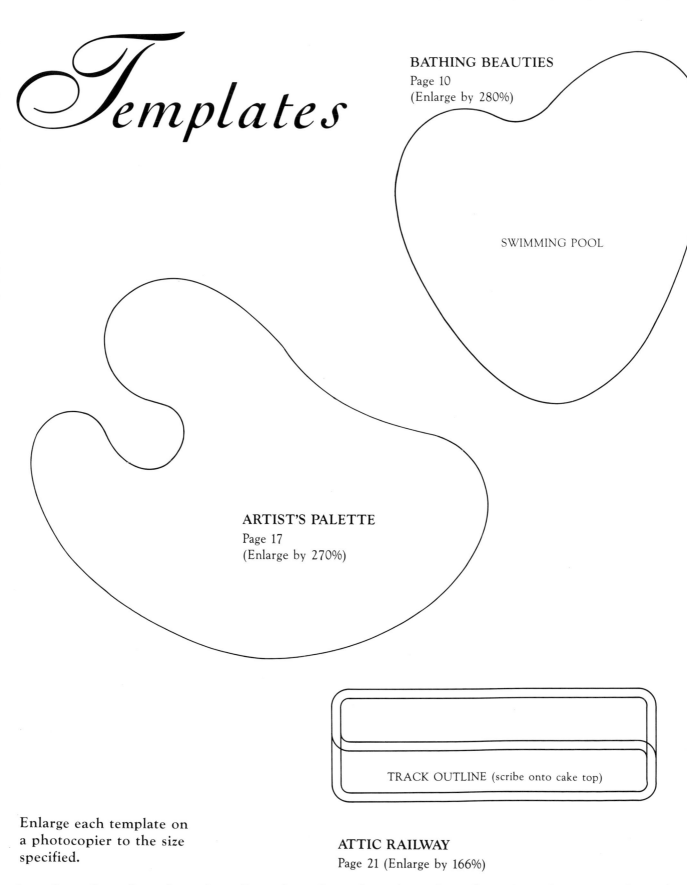

Templates

BATHING BEAUTIES
Page 10
(Enlarge by 280%)

SWIMMING POOL

ARTIST'S PALETTE
Page 17
(Enlarge by 270%)

TRACK OUTLINE (scribe onto cake top)

Enlarge each template on
a photocopier to the size
specified.

ATTIC RAILWAY
Page 21 (Enlarge by 166%)

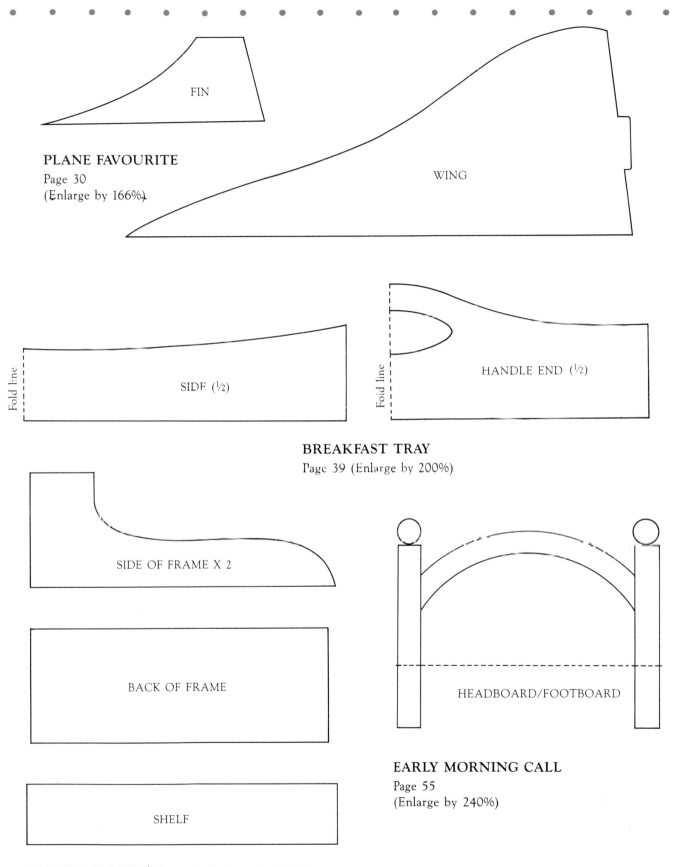

PLANE FAVOURITE
Page 30
(Enlarge by 166%)

FIN

WING

Fold line

SIDE (½)

Fold line

HANDLE END (½)

BREAKFAST TRAY
Page 39 (Enlarge by 200%)

SIDE OF FRAME X 2

BACK OF FRAME

HEADBOARD/FOOTBOARD

EARLY MORNING CALL
Page 55
(Enlarge by 240%)

SHELF

BATHROOM SINK Page 67 (Enlarge by 166%)

Index

Acknowledgements

The publishers would like to thank the following suppliers:

Cake Art Ltd
Venture Way,
Crown Estate,
Priorswood,
Taunton, TA2 8DE

Guy, Paul and Co. Ltd
Unit B4,
Foundry Way,
Little End Road,
Eaton Socon,
Cambs, PE19 3JH

Squires Kitchen
Squires House,
3 Waverley Lane,
Farnham,
Surrey, GU9 8BB

Anniversary House (Cake Decorations) Ltd
Unit 16,
Elliott Road,
West Howe Industrial Estate,
Bournemouth, BH11 8LZ